PHILOSOPHY
OF HISTORY

An Introduction

ROBERT PAUL MOHAN

PROFESSOR OF PHILOSOPHY
THE CATHOLIC UNIVERSITY OF AMERICA
WASHINGTON, D. C.

THE BRUCE PUBLISHING COMPANY / New York

To Lucy Riley Mohan
for all that she is

Library of Congress Catalog Card Number: 73-87994
Copyright © 1970 The Bruce Publishing Company
Made in the United States of America

CONTENTS

Foreword   vii

Introduction   xi

ONE   HISTORY AND THE PHILOSOPHY OF HISTORY   1
         History and Methodology
         Philosophy and History

TWO   CLASSICAL CYCLICISM   19
         The Greek Vision of Reality
         Greek Philosophical Thought and History

THREE   ST. AUGUSTINE AND LINEAR HISTORY   34
         The Jews and History
         Augustine's Philosophy of History
         Augustine's Immediate Influence

FOUR   VICO AND THE NEW SCIENCE   51
         Vico's Life and Background
         Cycle Theory

FIVE   HISTORY AND THE PHILOSOPHY OF PROGRESS   66
         Kant

        Early French Philosophers of Progress
        Turgot
        Saint-Simon
        Comte
        Marx

SIX   THE NEW CYCLICISM   88
        Nietzsche
        Danilevsky
        Spengler
        Sorokin

SEVEN IDEALISM AND HEGELIANISM   109
        Hegel
        Dilthey
        Croce

EIGHT TOYNBEE AND THE GOAL OF HISTORY   133
        The "New" Toynbee

NINE   THEOLOGY OF HISTORY AND THE AUGUSTINIAN 143
          SPIRIT
        Contemporary Theologies of History
        Teilhard de Chardin
        Maritain
        Dawson
        Marrou

TEN   PHILOSOPHY OF HISTORY AND THE CULTURAL 162
          MOOD

Epilogue   173

Index   175

FOREWORD

The philosophy of history is concerned with the essential nature of history and with the value and meaning of historical knowledge. In its analysis and synthesis it makes use of the data supplied by history itself. In a looser sense, the philosophy of history includes the theology of history, but, strictly speaking, the theology of history seeks the ultimate meaning of history outside and above history. The so-called philosophy of history of St. Augustine, for example, is not a philosophy of history, but a theology of history. The Greeks did not formulate a philosophy of history, unless one wishes to regard their cyclic conception of history as having a philosophical aspect. Judaeo-Christian thought, however, conceived of history in unilinear terms as the unfolding of the divine plan of God in time. History moves from the creation to the incarnation and from the incarnation to the end of the world and unity with God for eternity in heaven. This theological concept of history dominated Western thought from early Christianity to the Enlightenment.

Voltaire, Condorcet, and other representatives of the Enlightenment retained the Christian unilinear concept of historical development, but for the Christian theological concept they substituted the secular idea of progress toward a goal that they did not attempt to define. With the rise of the natural and

biological sciences in the nineteenth century, the philosophers
of history, influenced by the achievements and methods of these
sciences, sought to establish historical laws corresponding to
those of science. Comte especially, but Hegel also, reflected the
influence of the sciences in their elaborate philosophies of history. Comte was convinced that mankind could be improved by
the scientific application of historical laws. Hegel, by his emphasis on necessity in the stages of historical development, and by
his stress on becoming as a dynamic process in history, made a
special appeal to an age preoccupied with science and the new
theory of evolution. By his grandiose system, Hegel, in particular,
exercised an unusually wide influence on historical thought and
writing. A number of his terms like the "spirit of a nation," the
"*Zeitgeist*," and others are still in common use, although the
main tenets of his philosophy have been rejected.

In the second half of the nineteenth century and the early
twentieth, the majority of historians repudiated pretty much all
attempts at the philosophical explanation of history. Under the
general label of *Historismus* they stressed the importance of
thorough research and the solid establishment of historical facts.
It was maintained that the facts could speak for themselves and
that further generalization or interpretation was out of order.
However, *Historismus* in its characteristic form broke down.
Some historians became completely skeptical and questioned
the validity of all historical knowledge as such. But the majority
became convinced that an attempt at least should be made at
generalization or philosophical interpretation, however limited.
Moreover, there was a marked revival of the theological interpretation of history by a series of Christian writers like Karl Löwith,
Reinhold Niebuhr, and, especially, Christopher Dawson.

Oswald Spengler, though pessimistic in outlook and in part
an advocate of bizarre ideas, gave a new impetus to the rational-
istic-materialistic philosophy of history in his *Decline of the
West*. But it is Arnold Toynbee who has exercised the major influence on the revival of the philosophy of history by his *A Study
of History*, at once the most elaborate and comprehensive

work of its kind in historiography. Toynbee's ideas received
wide dissemination through D. C. Somervell's abridgements
of the *Study of History* which enjoyed phenomenal sales.
Without question, too, the tragic historical events of the twentieth century and their worldwide character, and the ever present thought that man through his mastery of atomic power
is now capable of destroying himself and all his achievements
over hundreds of thousands of years, have turned the minds of
scholars and of the general public as well to the whole question
of human values, and of the preservation of civilization. The
why of the tragic events of the contemporary period has led
scholars and statesmen to reconsider as never before the nature
and meaning of history.

Accordingly, Professor Mohan's *The Philosophy of History:
An Introduction* is a work that is as timely as it is valuable.
Based on long private study and on experience gained in the
teaching of courses on the philosophy of history to college and
university students, the book covers the history of the philosophy
of history in a clear, systematic, and readable form. The author
has been selective rather than exhaustive in his treatment. By
confining his exposition to typical and influential writers of
philosophies of history, he has been able to deal at sufficient
length with their leading ideas. It is a pleasure to note that Vico
has been covered with special care. Goethe with his customary
perspicacity had regarded him as an outstanding figure, but
otherwise his true significance has only been recognized in our
own times. The author has included a chapter on the theology
of history, giving the necessary prominence to St. Augustine
whose theology of history continues to be spoken of, although
erroneously, as a philosophy of history. Each chapter is followed
by a series of topics for further class discussion or seminars.

Professor Mohan's book should be read and studied not only
by students of history and philosophy, but also by the general
educated reader. Despite the shortcomings of most of the various
philosophies of history described, all were fruitful at least in
stimulating ideas and in leading readers to examine with greater

reflection the nature of history and of historical knowledge. The typical historian today not only feels the need of generalization but attempts to generalize and speculate on the meaning of history, if within well defined limits. If he avoids the term philosophy of history because of abuses connected with it, he does not hesitate to speak of "metahistory," which in many respects is simply a synonymous expression. Furthermore, a careful reading of Professor Mohan's book will enable the student to understand better the writings of the great historians themselves, for without exception they reveal a metahistorical, or even a definitely philosophical, outlook in their work, at least in practice.

Martin R. P. McGuire
Professor of Greek and Latin
and Ancient History
The Catholic University of America

INTRODUCTION

This volume is meant to be a serviceable text in an area which has been receiving increased attention in the academic community. Man, living in a cultural revolution and in a world of war, violence, and social upheaval, is impelled as never before to ask the hard questions of the meaning of historical existence. The book is arranged in terms of theory, problems, and personalities, on the general framework of cyclic, eschatological, and progressivist theories of historical explanation.

Because of the necessarily limited treatment of the subjects involved, the text should be used in conjunction with a number of current studies on particular personalities in the philosophy of history. Subjects for discussion and precise page references are given as background for suggested weekly seminars which might supplement regular class work.

To achieve the purpose for which this book was designed, most references given are to easily available English sources. Perhaps the best general references to work in the area done in the Western world are to be found in the *History and Theory* bibliographies of Professor John C. Rule, M. Nowicki, and Elie Halévy, published as Supplements 1, 3, and 7. Attention is also called to "Bibliography of Writings on Historiography and the Philosophy of History" by Martin Klein in *Generalization in the*

Writing of History, ed. Louis Gottschalk (Chicago: University of Chicago Press, 1963), pp. 213–247.

Books currently available in paperback are indicated by an asterisk.

The writer is particularly indebted to Arnold Toynbee, whose monumental *Study of History* first elicited his interest in the field, and whose thought-provoking comments to the author many years ago stimulated the present work. To Mary Libbey Culver and Margaret Neubeck of my staff, my sincere thanks for their characteristically devoted service.

Robert Paul Mohán
Professor of Philosophy
The Catholic University of America

CHAPTER ONE

HISTORY AND THE PHILOSOPHY

OF HISTORY

To study the philosophy of history is to examine first the nature of history and historical explanation. Is history the past event, the record of the event, or the general technique by which the event is recorded?

Is history the inquiry, the information sought, or the result of the inquiry? Is history as a science an open-ended experience in which the past must be continually reinterpreted to a changing present, or is the concept of a universally valid "definitive" history defensible? Is history a science at all, concerned as it is with the unique event rather than the abstract generality, or as Burckhardt observed, merely the record of facts which one age finds remarkable in another? What is the significance of theological or philosophical metahistory?

Do the facts of history speak for themselves, or are they agile performers whose conduct is determined by the epistemological presuppositions of the one who amasses them? Is the philosopher an intrusive element in history, trying to bring to a relatively objective science the classic ambiguities of philosophical explanation? Is there a meaning in history, or even discernible tendencies, or is any kind of historical objectivity as illusory as the crock of gold at the rainbow's end?

History as Art and Science

The late Morris Cohen, when accused of raising more questions than he could satisfactorily answer, was said to have remarked drily to his accuser: "It is not recorded that Hercules did anything more than clean out the Augean Stables!" Professor Cohen, incidentally, considered the philosophy of history the most neglected province of philosophy, and "the focal point of all applications of philosophy to life." [1] It may be that the historical imagination can indeed raise more questions than can be satisfactorily answered. But the questions are significant, and the answers have taken basic recognizable forms.

Popularly, we tend to think of history as the totality of human experience—"all we know about everything man has ever done, or thought, or hoped, or felt," as Professor James Harvey Robinson has phrased it. Or perhaps we think of history as humanity's diary, the record rather than the experience of mankind's most significant moments.

But history as early as the sixth century B.C. in Ionia was inquiry rather than recorded narrative. However, early writers, the "logographoi," were reproducing simple prose renditions of the traditions and legends of the towns and their people and places.[2]

> To them the ancient history was . . . the inquiry and statement, not the thing to be studied and recorded. It was not until modern times that the phenomena themselves were termed history. The history of the people originally meant the research and narrative of a historian, not the evolution of the nation. It meant a work of dealing with the subject, not the subject itself . . . The word "history" itself comes to us from these sixth-century Ionians

[1] Cf. Morris R. Cohen, *The Meaning of Human History* (LaSalle, Illinois: Open Court, 1961). The author considered this volume his chief work. Also cf. Christopher Dawson, "The Problem of Metahistory" in *Dynamics of World History* (New York: Doubleday, 1956), pp. 287–293.

[2] J. W. Thompson, *History of Historical Writing* (New York: Peter Smith, 1941), p. 22.

and is the name they gave to their achievement. It meant not the telling of a tale, but the search for knowledge and the truth. It was to them much what philosophy was to the later Athenians or science is to us. The historian was the critical inquirer.[3]

History as investigation is science, history as writing is an art form; and both as science and as art form it will be subject to the intellectual fashion of the cultural era that produces it and the personal skill of the historian who records it. Although there is no essential incompatibility between literary skill and historical truth, the historian's primary aim is the past actuality itself, investigated critically and scientifically. If he can tell his story with the literary skill of an Herodotus, he is twice blessed.[4]

Arthur Schlesinger, Jr. observes: "All the elements of artistic form are as organic in historical as in any other kind of literary composition. . . . Written history, after all, is the application of an aesthetic vision to a welter of facts; and both the weight

[3] J. T. Shotwell, *The History of History* (New York: Columbia University Press 1939), pp. 5, 8; cf. also H. E. Barnes, *A History of Historical Writing* (New York: Dover, 1962), p. 26. Barnes says of the Hebrew historical tradition: "The first Hebrew historical writing, which marks the earliest appearance of the true historical narrative of which any record has anywhere been preserved, is to be found in the work of the uncertain authors of the 'Jahvist' sources of the Pentateuch, Joshua, the Books of Samuel, and the opening of the First Book of Kings." *Ibid.*, p. 22.

[4] A succinct summary of the problem of the scientific character of history is found in Gilbert J. Garraghan's *A Guide to Historical Method* (New York: Fordham University Press, 1951), pp. 37–42. Cf. also "What the Historian Thinks He Knows" in H. Stuart Hughes' brilliant little book, *History as Art and as Science* (New York: Harper & Row, 1964), pp. 1–21; Sir Isaiah Berlin, "The Concept of Scientific History," *History and Theory*, Vol. I, No. 1, 1960, pp. 1–31. R. G. Collingwood observes: "History, then, is a science of a special kind. It is a science whose business is to study events not accessible to our observations, and to study these events inferentially, arguing to them from something else which is accessible to our observation, and which the historian calls 'evidence' for the events in which he is interested." *The Idea of History* (Oxford: Oxford University Press, 1946), pp. 251–252. In an earlier passage he pictures history as having four characteristics. It is scientific in that it begins by asking questions, humanistic by centering those questions on the acts of man at determinate times, rational, by judging answers on the basis of evidence, and self revelatory, by telling man what he is by telling man what he has done. Cf. p. 18.

and the vitality of an historical work depend on the quality of the vision." [5]

Marrou contends that all the great historians have to be artists with words lest the precious cargo of knowledge be damaged in transit. History, of course, is more than private recollection or random reminiscence; it is intelligent inquiry, the sifting and organization of evidence, interpretation and presentation, in a fashion that exhibits craftsmanship and skill. Marrou says: "If Ranke . . . is honored by us as the first modern historian, in the sense in which we are using the word, it is because he was able to combine the penetration and subtlety or an inquiring mind and the breadth of vision of a philosophic mind with the great skill of a master of his language." [6]

But no matter how great his skill, the historian's tale is never told. Definitive history can never be absolute or complete until the human experience itself is complete. For even when the facts are relatively well known (and they never can be completely known), they will have to be retold and reinterpreted for generation after generation, each of which poses new questions from the uniqueness of its own historical experience. A scholar's inquiry, reflection, and writing will invariably be subjectively and historically conditioned.

John Courtney Murray, in a fine essay on natural law theory, observed:

> But history, as any history book shows, does change what I have called the human reality. It evokes situations that never happened before. It calls into being relationships that had not existed. It involves human life in an increasing multitude of institutions of all kinds, which proliferate in response to new human needs and desires, as well as in consequence of the creative possibilities that are inexhaustibly resident in human freedom. [7]

[5] Arthur Schlesinger, Jr., as quoted in Henry Steele Commager, *The Nature and study of History* (Columbus, Ohio: Charles E. Merrill, 1965), p. 6.

[6] Henri-Irénée Marrou, *The Meaning of History* (Baltimore: Helicon, 1966), p. 295.

[7] John Courtney Murray, S.J., "Natural Law and Public Consensus," in *Natural Law and Modern Society*, intr. by John Cogley (Cleveland: World, 1966), p. 66.

Carl Becker's observation that every man is his own historian is reflective of the further subjectivity of unique personalities working in the same general environment. It has been said that St. Augustine looked at Roman history from the point of view of an early Christian; Tillemont, from that of a seventeenth-century Frenchman; Gibbon from that of an eighteenth-century Englishman; Mommsen, from that of a nineteenth-century German.

HISTORY AND METHODOLOGY

A further problem is that of the methodology employed by the historian to articulate his unique vision of reality. The changes in research over the years have liberated the historian from too exclusive a dependence on documents. In his methodology he will devise new and ingenious ways of quizzing the past. As Professor Lynn White has observed, the tremendous growth of the natural sciences has put novel power tools in the historian's kit. He cites as an example the development of scintillation counters developed in 1953 at the Universities of Manitoba and Chicago which supposedly date plant or animal materials over a 44,000 year period with a maximum error possibility of thirty-seven years.[8] In the freshness of inquiry, in the enrichment of historical knowledge itself, and in interpreting the results anew to another generation, the historian will be performing a function that he knows will have to be re-done again for his own or another's changing generation.

History as recorded actuality is primarily *human* history, experienced or recorded from selected sources, unquestionably reflective of the personal value judgments of the historian, and concerned with the individual only to the degree to which he

[8] Lynn White, Jr., "The Changing Past," *Harper's Magazine*, 39 (1954), pp. 29–30.

affects the collectivity.[9] Bernheim brings out this emphasis when he defines history as the knowledge of the development of human beings in their activities as social beings. Mandelbaum too considers history a *"Kulturwissenschaft,"* or a "study of human activities in their societal context and with their societal implications."

That history is primarily human history is not to contrast it so much with the philosophy of nature as to minimize the Hegelian concept of the political state as the proper absolute of historical inquiry. History concerns not only the "what" of what actually occurred, but also the "why," despite the fact that the more factually-oriented historian feels more at home with a detached narrative of the facts rather than with causal explanations of the facts.[10]

The positivist in history, despite his unquestioned contribution to critical method, labors under the delusion of objectivity when he thinks that facts speak for themselves. For until facts are assembled into a meaningful context, they are "the mere dross of history" as Lord Macaulay calls them, inert statistics, and their very selection from a larger body of facts indicates a subjective if unacknowledged value judgment. H. Stuart Hughes expresses this idea well:

I have learned that the result of the historian's efforts to be detached has usually been the very opposite of what anyone would

---

[9] Cf. William H. Dray, *Philosophy of History* (Englewood Cliffs, N.J.: Prentice-Hall, 1964), p. 4; Maurice Mandelbaum, *The Problem of Historical Knowledge* (New York: Harper, 1938), p. 10; R. G. Collingwood, *The Idea of History* (Oxford: Oxford University Press, 1946), pp. 9, 205–231; W. H. Walsh, *An Introduction to Philosophy of History* (London: Hillary, 1951), p. 30; G. J. Renier, *History Its Purpose and Method* (New York: Hillary, 1965), pp. 189–204; Ernest Gellner, "Holism versus Individualism in History and Sociology," in Patrick Gardiner (ed.), *Theories of History* (Glencoe: The Free Press, 1959), pp. 489–503.

[10] Narrative history is but one type of historical record; didactic history attempts to draw lessons from historical experience; and genetic history considers the evolutionary and developmental character of events and the complicated causation involved. Cf. Fritz Stern (ed.), *The Varieties of History* (New York: Meridian, 1959); and Henry Steele Commager, *op. cit.,* Chapter Two: "The Varieties of History," pp. 15–26. Professor Commager suggests that the traditional (but not final or authoritative) patterns of history are the chronological, the geographical, the political, the cultural, the institutional, and the biological.

call great history. It has been bloodless history, with no clear focus, arising from antiquarian curiosity rather than from deep personal concern, and shot through with metaphysical and moral assumptions that are all the more insidious for being artfully concealed.[11]

This does not mean that a kind of historical objectivity is impossible; it does mean that history does not possess the same kind of objectivity as the empirical sciences. Facts never totally disengage themselves from the person who records them, and the historical event or happening is not an independently existing entity. It has been surgically excised from its cultural context so that it may be given a closer look by an interested observer. As Professor Walsh says: "Impartial history, so far from being an ideal, is a downright impossibility." [12] And Marrou observes that the historian who primly asserts that he ignores philosophy and cultivates his own little garden is really lowering himself to the status of an unskilled laborer.[13]

PHILOSOPHY AND HISTORY

If the philosopher has invaded history, what is the extent of the invasion? Is it true that historians do not have great philosophical needs? Or, as Croce has suggested, are the two disciplines inseparable? If, as Norman Sykes has said, ". . . the straitest school of scientific historians find it impossible to

[11] H. Stuart Hughes, op. cit., p. 96. Carl Becker, in an address to the American Historical Association in 1926, observed: "The simple historical fact turns out to be not a hard, cold something with clear outline and measurable pressure like a brick. It is, so far as we can know it, only a symbol, a simple statement which is a generalization of a thousand and one simpler facts which we do not for the moment care to use, and this generalization itself we cannot use apart from the wider facts and generalizations it symbolizes. . . . Perhaps the safest thing we can say about a symbol is not that it is in fact either true or false, but only more or less appropriate."

[12] W. H. Walsh, op. cit., p. 20. Cf. also C. V. Langlois and C. Seignobos, Introduction to the Study of History (New York: Holt, 1925), p. 287; and C. A. Beard, "Written History as an Act of Faith," The American Historical Review, 39 (1934), p. 228.

[13] Henri Marrou, op. cit., p. 11.

restrain their steps from divagations into the pasture of philosophy," how much more interpretative and subjective is the
historian whose orientation is frankly philosophic? [14]

There are fashions in thought as there are fashions in clothes,
and since the term "philosophy of history" was used for the first
time (as a systematic interpretation of universal history by which
it is invested with some unified and ultimate meaning), the
popularity of this area of inquiry has varied depending on the
cultural mood.[15]

Eighteenth-century rationalist historians like Gibbon and
Voltaire were frankly interpretative; nineteenth-century historians, reflecting the empiricist's preoccupation with the measurable and factual and influenced by the achievements and
methods of the natural and biological sciences, tended more
often than not to articulate the positivist mood.

The twentieth century has been much more sympathetic to
interpretative history as evidenced by the popularity of such
works as those of Spengler, Sorokin, Toynbee, Dawson, and
Teilhard de Chardin. A world in crisis tends to be receptive of
theories which attempt to explain human experience in its
totality.

As regards the term "philosophy of history," Juan Donoso
Cortés refers in his *Ensayo* to St. Augustine's *City of God* as a
"Catholic philosophy of history." In his essay on Vico, however,
he refers to Bossuet as the "first philosopher of history." [16] Vico
himself is called by H. P. Adams "the founder of philosophy of
history." [17] Karl Löwith, in referring to a period of crisis at the

[14] Benedetto Croce: "There is neither philosophy nor history, nor history of
philosophy, but history which is philosophy and intrinsic to history." *History, Its
Theory and Practice* (New York: Russell, 1937), p. 83.

[15] For an analysis of what might be called the cultural climate and its influence,
cf. H. Stuart Hughes, *Consciousness and Society* (New York: Vintage, 1958),
and the same author's *Oswald Spengler* (New York: Charles Scribner's Sons,
1952), pp. 14–26. Goethe observes: "What you call the spirit of the age is in
reality one's own spirit, in which the age is mirrored."

[16] Cf. T. Neill, "Juan Donoso Cortés; History and 'Prophecy'." *The Catholic
Historical Review*, 40 (1955), pp. 392–393.

[17] H. Adams, *The Life and Writings of Giambattista Vico* (London: George
Allen & Unwin, 1935).

end of the seventeenth century, when, as he says, "Providence was replaced by progress," insists that Voltaire's *Essay on the Manners and Mind of Nations* (1756) is the first philosophy of history; and Löwith considers this event the inauguration of an epoch of historical evaluation basically anti-religious.[18] Marie Collins Swabey rejects this identification of philosophical history with figures like Voltaire, Montesquieu, or Kant, and prefers to consider the problem in terms of general orientation.[19] W. H. Walsh, in his *Introduction in Philosophy of History*, claims that philosophy of history first gained recognition in 1784 with the publication of the first part of Herder's *Ideas for a Philosophical History of Mankind*.[20] Collingwood maintains that the name at least "was invented by Voltaire, who meant by it no more than critical or scientific history." [21] Shirley Jackson Case concedes that Voltaire may be said to have coined the phrase, but considers that the technique of evaluation involved was current in the thought of the ancient Hebrews.[22] Raymond Aron's use of the term is more like that of Case and Swabey. He is concerned with a philosophical conception of the historical process as a whole in opposition to positivism and *"rationalisme scientiste"*.[23] Professor Manuel considers philosophies of histories as historical worldviews which magically mirror the mind and sensibility of the ages in which they are composed in such a way that the former image remains after the reality changes.[24]

From such a variety of opinion some basic facts emerge. The name, at least, originates with Voltaire, who summarizes his

[18] K. Löwith, *Meaning in History* (Chicago: University of Chicago Press, 1950), p. 104.
[19] M. Swabey, *The Judgment of History* (New York: Philosophical Library, 1954), p. 175.
[20] W. H. Walsh, *An Introduction to Philosophy of History* (London: Hillary, 1951), p. 11.
[21] R. Collingwood, *op. cit.*, p. 1.
[22] S. Case, *The Christian Philosophy of History* (Chicago: University of Chicago Press, 1943), p. 16.
[23] R. Aron, *Introduction to the Philosophy of History* (Boston: Beacon, 1948), p. 12.
[24] Frank E. Manuel, *Shapes of Philosophical History* (Stanford, California: Stanford University Press, 1965), p. 5.

position in the dictum: *Il faut écrire l'histoire en philosophe* (One must be a philosopher to write history.) Second, not all writers on the subject introduce theology as a consideration. And finally, there is no general agreement as to the role philosophy should play in historical interpretation. This difference is reflected in an oscillation between extremes of factual and philosophic history that seems to take place over the years.[25]

A distinction is to be made too between speculative and critical philosophies of history. Speculative philosophy of history (which Professor Dray feels to be going out of fashion) seeks to find a patterned significance in the historical process of a whole. Critical philosophy of history scrutinizes the epistemological presuppositions of the historian, analyzes the nature of historical knowledge and objectivity, and, in the spirit of the time, weighs the possibility and limitation of philosophical terminology.[26]

It has been suggested that any historian giving the "long look" to the richness of reality will record in one of four classical patterns.[27] The first is the idealist pattern of Leopold von Ranke —the attempt to write history "as it actually was" by an intuitive grasp of the meaning of the historical event; the second is the positivist attempt to reduce historical data to an atomized collection of facts following the technique of the quantitative sciences; the third is the neo-idealist attempt (such as that of Croce and Dilthey) to understand, by a subjective re-thinking of the past, events already irrevocably acted out on the stage of history; the fourth is the neo-positivist pattern of the critical professional historian which concerns itself primarily with

[25] Robert Paul Mohan, "Is There a Philosophy of History?", *The New Scholasticism*, 30, 4 (October 1956), pp. 462–463.
[26] Cf. William H. Dray, *Philosophy of History* (Englewood Cliffs, N. J.: Prentice-Hall, 1964), p. 2; and W. H. Walsh, *op. cit.*, pp. 13–28. Professor Arthur C. Danto, influenced by C. I. Lewis and A. J. Ayer, has written perhaps the most significant book on the philosophy of history from the viewpoint of the analytic philosopher. He examines particularly the validity of language in historical narrative. *Analytical Philosophy of History* (Cambridge: Cambridge University Press, 1965).
[27] H. Stuart Hughes, *op. cit.*, pp. 7–17.

methodology, measurable processes and verifiable data, but which does not exclude interpretative judgment.[28]

The philosophy of history itself is really as old as man's attempts to see significance in his earthly existence. As theologians, philosophers, anthropologists, sociologists, and even economists are involved in the general area of inquiry that has come to be known as the philosophy of history, it would be well to distinguish the specific approaches.

1. The first great category of historical interpretation is classical cyclicism which envisions an eternal universe featuring a continuous recurrence of historical experience. Toynbee considers cyclicism to have had its probable origin in ancient Chaldean astronomy, but it derived much of its force in the ancient world as an intellectually naïve extrapolation from a world of nature that exhibited observably recurrent daily and seasonal changes. Linear creationism was practically unknown in the ancient world, and even the *Timaeus* of Plato and scattered references in Epicurus make no case for a genuine creation in the Jewish or Christian sense of the term.[29] St. Augustine's *City of God* is not only a classical defense of Christianity against the charge that it was responsible (by infidelity to Rome's gods) for the sack of Rome under Alaric in 410. It is also Christianity's most famous protest against a cyclicism that would confine history within itself in a series of endless repetitions. Ancient cyclicism had its psychological counterpart in the theories of

[28] Lest undue emphasis seem to be given the idealist positions, it might be remembered that the past exists only in our present reflection of what has already occurred, not as a muted present whose voice and spirit can be evoked at the will of the inquirer. Collingwood phrases it: "It is the past as residually preserved in the present that is alone knowable." *Essays in the Philosophy of History* (Austin, Texas: University of Texas Press, 1965), p. 100.

[29] *Meaning in History* (Chicago: University of Chicago Press, 1949), p. 248. Karl Löwith cites the main sources for the classical view of eternal recurrence as Fragments 30, 31, 51, 63, 67, 68 of Heraclitus; Fragment 115 of Empedocles; most of the myths of Plato; Aristotle's *Metaphysics*, xii, 8, *On the Heavens* i, 3 and 4; Fragment 51, Eudemus; *Ep. ad Lucilium* 24, Seneca. Early Christian sources are Justin's *Dialog with Trypho* i, introduction, and Origen's *Against Celsus* iv, 67 v. 20, *De Principiis* ii, 3.

metempsychosis which pictured successive psychic existences in historically repetitive patterns.

2. The second great area of inquiry for the philosopher of history is providential history—such as that written by St. Augustine and Bossuet. Providential history sees the historical process initiated by a divine creative act and proceeding meaningfully to a conclusion. It is teleological, but not deterministic, as man's free will is a part of the disposition of providence rather than a competing dynamic principle outside it. Such a theologically-oriented eschatology is not, strictly speaking, a philosophy at all, but as it is broadly interpretative, it is included for consideration in most works in philosophy of history.

Christopher Dawson quite correctly observes that the Christian vision of history is essentially theological in character, reflecting an integral part of divine revelation rather than a philosophical effort elaborated by Christian scholars. Augustinian history is inevitably universal, and, as it envisages an eternal goal beyond the temporal order, it is metahistorical. As Collingwood has pointed out, Greco-Roman ecumenical history is not universal in the Christian sense, because it has the particularistic center of gravity which is Greece or Rome.[30] Augustinian history will have a pivotal event, the Incarnation, to which the pre-Christian era moves, and by which the post-Incarnation era is transfigured. Eusebius will see in his *Preparatio Evangelica* human events as preparatory to the coming of Christ, and consequent events as transfigured by that event. The Christian vision of history involves a restructuring of thought as well as a liberation from cyclicism. Although a secular scholar like Bury sees in providential history external control rather than liberation, St. Augustine's *City of God* does herald a new linear dimension in historical experience, in which free human activity, moving into

---

[30] Cf. Collingwood's treatment of the characteristics of Christian historiography in *The Idea of History*, pp. 45–56. A portion of this treatment is to be found in Alan and Barbara Donagan *Philosophy of History* (New York: Macmillan, 1965), pp. 23–25.

an unknown future, acquires a unique meaning not destined for inevitable repetition.[31]

3. A third species considered in a philosophy of history is a type of interpretative history that claims the existence of laws or keys that would reveal the metaphysic of the historical process.[32] In its extreme form it either replaces causation itself by destiny (as in Spengler) or overemphasizes single causative elements, and sees all history determined by such factors as race, geography, climate, and economics, or given new impulses and directions by what Collingwood calls "apocalyptic" events— such as the Renaissance, the invention of printing, the Reformation, the Enlightenment of the eighteenth century, the French Revolution, or the socio-political liberal movements of the nineteenth century.

Interpretative extremism also features history as prophecy, for if the major cosmic impulse, deterministic in character, can be sufficiently identified, then the future as well as the past can be expected to yield its secrets. Needless to say, it is this unwarranted gnosticism in history to which the critical historian most vehemently and justifiably objects. He may consider the insights of a Spengler ingeniously formulated and interestingly reflective of a deeply-felt personal version of the historical process, but he is understandably hesitant to accord them objectivity. But the critical historian, particularly if he ignores epistemological antecedents (consciously adopted or inadvertently assumed) and is inordinately distracted by the merely factual, can forget, as

---

[31] Cf. J. B. Bury, *The Idea of Progress* (New York: Macmillan, 1955), pp. 21–22. Bury does admit that "Christian theology constructed a synthesis which for the first time attempted to give a definite meaning to the whole course of human events . . ." *Ibid.* He also calls providence an "organizing conception" in the thought of Augustine and Bossuet. *Ibid.* p. 158. W. H. Walsh speaks of such a technique as "colligating" events under appropriate conceptions. Cf. *An Introduction to Philosophy of History*, p. 62.

[32] For an analysis of historical causation, cf. Morton White, *Foundations of Historical Knowledge* (New York: Harper and Row, 1965), chs. 4, 5; Section III, pp. 156–197; Raymond Aron, *op. cit.*; and Sir Isaiah Berlin, "Historical Inevitability" in Hans Meyerhoff (ed.), *The Philosophy of History in Our Time* (New York: Doubleday, 1959), pp. 249–269.

Ernest Bernheim has suggested, that the philosophy of history is by no means superfluous luxury for the historian.

4. A fourth possibility is interpretative history or history "integrally taken," non-deterministic in character, which, while recognizing the unpredictable character of free human choice, nevertheless sees certain discernible patterns or trends in the historical process as a whole. Jacques Maritain speaks of axiomatic formulas by which he means certain formulas which reveal the endurance of certain basic relations or fundamental characteristics. He distinguishes these functional laws from what he calls typological or vectoral laws—more particularized descriptions of historical growth and development which exhibit a typical direction.[33] It would indeed seem to be a worthwhile enterprise to study meaningful patterns or cultural unities which the richness of historical material may exhibit, while recognizing the inability of even the most perceptive of minds to predict a future determined by the unknown decisions of free men.

5. A fifth category of the philosophy of history is simply philosophically-oriented history which, while not neglecting the factual, is more preoccupied with relations and causes, general as well as specific, epistemological positions antecedent to investigation, and a philosophy of man with particular emphasis on human freedom. This critical type of philosophical history, exemplified by Collingwood's work, is a matter of general orientation.

6. A final area of inquiry in the philosophy of history is held by the secular philosophies of progress produced by the rationalism of the eighteenth and nineteenth centuries. History and cultural institutions came to be judged in the light of an ascending progressive evolution. Nietzsche was quite correct in seeing the philosophies of progress (which he despised) as a "trivialization" and secularization of Christian linearism (which he also despised). But the new Jerusalem of the progressivists was an

---

[33] Jacques Maritain, On the Philosophy of History (New York: Charles Scribner's Sons, 1957).

earthly city that envisioned no transcendent goal. As has been generally observed, this trend to the secular had been abetted by both Renaissance and Reformation, and by the scientism of empiricists desirous of extending natural science to philosophy. Rectilinear progress had its psychological variant in the turn-of-the-century Couéism which assured increasingly insecure man that every day in every way he was getting better and better. General theories of progress are associated particularly with the writings of Fontenelle, the Abbé of Saint Pierre, the Marquis de Condorcet, Voltaire, Fourier, Saint Simon, Turgot, Darwin, and Comte. Latent in progressivistic theory is the idea that progress is a law of nature, and that such a law applies both to the processes of the natural order and the cultural development of man. The theory finds much to substantiate it in the order of technology where the accumulated intellectual capital of the past is at the service of contemporary use and experimentation. Academic capital is added to in each successive generation, although it is questionable to suggest that available knowledge is acquired by successive generations with increasing skill.

Voltaire's prejudice in favor of contemporary history and the belief that history exhibited a constant progress from a barbarous primitive era to his own day was not only reflective of an arbitrary conviction that the only meaningful history was modern history, but it was also the consequence of a limited knowledge of the age that was held to be primitive.

Nicholas Berdyaev (*The Meaning of History*) was perhaps the progressivist's most formidable modern adversary. He considered the philosophy of progress a secularized messianism, a divinization of the future at the expense of the past and present that has not the slightest philosophic, scientific, or moral justification.[34] But the idea of progress was a comfortable and optimistic illusion that endured until the early years of the twentieth century when the static and peaceful Newtonian universe began to collapse

[34] Nicholas Berdyaev, *The Meaning of History* (London: Geoffrey Bles, 1949), Chapter X.

as empirical science expanded its frontiers, and a devastating worldwide conflict reminded man that he was capable of going in more than a forward direction.

Granted that one can approach the philosophy of history in different ways, it is nevertheless possible to reduce the problem to even more basic categories in the light of which leading personalities in the field may be considered.

The first category in this further division is that of classical cyclicism already referred to; the second is that of linear eschatological direction; and the third is that of secular futurism which finds historical expression in the philosophies of progress. Hughes and Manuel would reduce the alternative ways of viewing historical experience to the cyclical and the progressive, combining Christian linearism and secular futurism into one progressivist outlook.[35]

A final observation might be made about the universality of the historical enterprise. As the historian's point of view is inevitably perspectival, so the object of the historian's inquiry is almost inevitably parochial. The merit of a Spengler and a Toynbee is not that they have written either exhaustively or well about non-European civilization, but that they have at least tried to look beyond a limited cultural horizon.

SUGGESTED READINGS

I. THE NATURE OF HISTORICAL EXPLANATION

Morris Cohen, *The Meaning of Human History, LaSalle, Illinois: Open Court, 1961, Chapter One: "The Task of the Historian," pp. 3–34.

R. G. Collingwood, Essays in the Philosophy of History, Austin, Texas: University of Texas Press, 1965, "The Limits of Historical Knowledge," pp. 90–103.

Henry Steele Commager, The Nature and the Study of History, Columbus, Ohio: C. E. Merrill, 1966, Chapter One: "The Nature of History," pp. 1–14.

[35] Frank Manuel, Shapes of Philosophical History (Stanford, California: Stanford University Press, 1965), p. 5; H. Stuart Hughes, Oswald Spengler (New York: Charles Scribner's Sons, 1952), p. 28.

Benedetto Croce, *History, Its Theory and Practice*, trans. by Douglas Ainslie, New York: Russell, 1937. Part I "Theory of Historiography," pp. 11-164.

M. C. D'Arcy, *The Meaning and Matter of History*, New York: Meridian, 1959, pp. 13-62.

William H. Dray, *Philosophy of History*, Englewood Cliffs, New Jersey: Prentice Hall, 1964, Chapter Two: "Historical Understanding," pp. 4-20.

Charles Frankel, "Explanation and Interpretation in History" in *Theories of History*, ed. Patrick Gardiner, Glencoe, Illinois: Free Press, 1959, pp. 408-427.

Gilbert Garraghan, *A Guide to Historical Method*, New York: Fordham University Press, 1961, Chapter One: "The Meaning of History," pp. 3-32.

H. Stuart Hughes, *History As Art and As Science*, New York: Harper & Row, 1964, Chapter One: "What the Historian Thinks He Knows," pp. 1-21.

Johan Huizinga, "A Definition of the Concept of History" in *Philosophy and History*, ed. Raymond Klibansky, H. J. Paton, New York: Peter Smith, 1963, pp. 1-10.

Henri Marrou, *The Meaning of History*, Baltimore: Helicon, 1966, Chapter One: "History as Knowledge," pp. 29-52; and "The Nature of Historical Work," pp. 287-299.

G. J. Renier, *History, Its Purpose and Method*, New York: Hillary, 1965, Part One: "What is History?" pp. 13-86.

II. HISTORICAL OBJECTIVITY

Raymond Aron, "Relativism in History" in *The Philosophy of History in Our Time*, ed. Hans Meyerhoff, New York: Doubleday, 1959, pp. 153-161.

Harry Elmer Barnes, *A History of Historical Writing*, New York: Dover, 1962, pp. 266-275.

Christopher Blake, "Can History Be Objective?" in *Theories of History*, ed. P. Gardiner, Glencoe, Illinois: Free Press, 1959, pp. 329-343.

Marc Bloch, *The Historian's Craft*, New York: Knopf, 1953, Chapter Four: "Historical Analysis," pp. 138-189.

Arthur C. Danto, *Analytical Philosophy of History*, London: Cambridge University Press, 1965, Chapter Six: "Evidence and Historical Relativism," pp. 88-111.

William H. Dray, *Philosophy of History*, Englewood Cliffs, New Jersey: Prentice-Hall, 1964, Chapter Three: "Historical Objectivity," pp. 21-40.

Maurice Mandelbaum, "Objectivism in History" in *Philosophy and History*, ed. Sidney Hook, New York: New York University Press, 1963, pp. 43-58.

F. Medicus, "On the Objectivity of Historical Knowledge," in *Philos-

18   PHILOSOPHY OF HISTORY

ophy and History, ed. R. Klibansky, H. J. Paton, New York: Peter Smith, 1966, pp. 137–158.

Ernest Nagel, "The Logic of Historical Analysis" in *The Philosophy of History in Our Time*, ed. Hans Meyerhoff, New York: Doubleday, 1959, pp. 203–215.

W. H. Walsh, *An Introduction to Philosophy of History*, London: Hillary, 1951, Chapter Five: "Can History be Objective?", pp. 94–118.

Morton G. White, "Can History Be Objective?" in *The Philosophy of History in Our Time*, ed. Hans Meyerhoff, New York: Doubleday, 1959, pp. 188–202.

III. HISTORY AS SCIENCE

Isaiah Berlin, "The Concept of Scientific History" in *Philosophical Analysis and History*, ed. William H. Dray, New York: Harper and Row, 1966, pp. 5–53.

Marc Bloch, *The Historian's Craft*, New York: Knopf, 1953, Ch. II: "Historical Observation," pp. 48–78.

Morris R. Cohen, *The Meaning of Human History*, LaSalle, Illinois: Open Court, 1961, Ch. II: "Metaphysics and History," pp. 35–43.

R. G. Collingwood, *The Idea of History*, Oxford: Oxford University Press, 1946, pp. 249–282; *Essays in the Philosophy of History*, Austin, Texas: University of Texas, 1965, pp. 23–33.

C. G. Hempel, "Explanation in Science and History," in *Philosophical Analysis and History*, ed. William H. Dray, New York: Harper and Row, 1966, pp. 95–126.

H. Stuart Hughes, *History As Art and As Science*, New York: Harper and Row, 1964, Ch. II: "History, the Humanities, and Anthropological Change," pp. 22–41.

Maurice Mandelbaum, *The Problem of Historical Knowledge*, New York: Harper and Row, 1938, "The Field of History," pp. 1–14.

Jacques Maritain, *On the Philosophy of History*, New York: Charles Scribner's Sons, 1957, pp. 2–19.

Henri Marrou, *The Meaning of History*, Baltimore: Helicon, 1966, Ch. I: "History as Knowledge," pp. 29–52.

Frederick J. Teggart, *Theory and Processes of History*, Berkeley, California: University of California Press, 1962, Ch. XIII: "The Method of Science," pp. 155–167.

W. H. Walsh, "The Limits of Scientific History" in *Philosophical Analysis and History*, William H. Dray (ed.), New York: Harper and Row, 1966, pp. 54–75.

CHAPTER TWO

CLASSICAL CYCLICISM

Contemporary man, be he a devout theist or a happy pagan, tends to look upon a cyclic view of history with simultaneous disbelief and curiosity. With disbelief, because of his psychological repugnance for the constrictive circle which confines humanity to an endless repetition of triumphs and tragedies in which freedom is meaningless and a genuine future non-existent; with curiosity, because of his wonder that such an alien thought structure could have so completely dominated the ancient world, not only in the early Ionian period, but in the Platonic, Aristotelian, Stoic, and Epicurean Greek and Roman worlds of a later period.

The Greek Vision of Reality

The Greek did not think of freedom as the capacity to choose without constraint as a maker of history, but as the recognition of the necessity of an endlessly repetitive world. This theme first occurs in myth, that allusive type of story which gave pre-scientific man a vivid, if not logically coherent, explanation of the mysteries of his world. Fate hovered over the most ambitious of human enterprises; triumph, prideful arrogance, and destruction were realities known to the noblest as well as the meanest of men, but always as part of a total and by no means depressing experience. History could be endured, because, like the physical world, it was necessary.

It was ultimately in philosophy that Greek art and thought was unified in an integrated vision of reality. Greek curiosity sought the underlying law of all reality, linking all disparate existences into an anthropocentric worldview deeply rooted in historical experience. The Greek was the man at home in the world, seeking the noble courage of *areté* in the various worlds of the poet, statesman, and thinker.[1] The same mind that saw beauty and meaning in a balanced view of the artistic part and whole viewed endless repetition in history with serenity, while for Nietzsche in later centuries eternal recurrence, which was renewed so prominently in his thought, was to be a frightful and terrifying burden. The Greek had his fears, but he lived within what Professor Zimmern calls "concentric circles of loyalty" that gave him a sense of permanence.

The figures of the great tragic artists, Aeschylus, Sophocles, and Euripides are not great because they are free in a contemporary sense of the word, or because they make history; they are great because of the luminous quality of their insights, the aristocratic courage and nobility of their reactions in an ordered universe that they would think it impious and presumptuous to change. Sophocles says in *Antigone* (456):

> "Tell me, when was custom born,
> Yester eve or yester year?"
> "Days and years she knoweth not.
> She was always here."[2]

---

[1] Cf. Werner Jaeger, *Paideia, The Ideals of Greek Culture* (New York: Oxford University Press, 1945), Ch. I, "Nobility and Areté," pp. 3–14; C. M. Bowra, *The Greek Experience* (New York: New American Library, 1957), Ch. II, "The Heroic Outlook," pp. 32–53; and Alfred Zimmern, *The Greek Commonwealth* (New York: Oxford University Press, 1956), Ch. II, "Custom, or Rule of the Family," pp. 61–75.

[2] The contemporary Swiss dramatist, Max Frisch, in his play, *The Chinese Wall*, deals interestingly with the recurrence problem. The hero asks: "Is this what history means that man's mistakes keep repeating endlessly?" And in the last scene the stage is prepared again for the first act. "The farce is going to start all over again," the audience is told.

Oedipus is certainly not an evil man, and if tragedy is pain transmuted into exaltation by the alchemy of poetry, then in his very agony he savors of the tragic greatness of life.[3] But Oedipus' pains are not providentially directed to any metahistorical goal. They have their meaning and nobility, but it is not the meaning that the religious man sees in terms of an ultimate beatific vision, nor the meaning that the secular progressivist sees in the sociopolitical possibilities of an enlightened tomorrow. The Greek saw history as a circle, not a line; his was a revolt against concrete historical time, a "nostalgia for a periodical return to the mythical time of the beginning of things, to the 'Great Time.'"[4] In ancient thought in general, reality itself is acquired through repetition, the primitive tending to repeat or imitate a permanently existing model or archetype, suggestive of a Platonic ontology.

The ancient's rejection of time also takes the form of religious sacrifice which suspends the flow of linear time, as it were, and captures the meaning of a primordial and timelessly repeated event. He who sacrifices isolates himself from the profane time to capture a timeless universal value. He has a deep sense of the numinous, that is, of those qualities of fear and wonderment before the awe-inspiring majesty of the "Wholly Other." Rite becomes a fragment of eternity. Sacred time is recoverable and indefinitely repeatable, making possible an eternal present. When man loses his religious sense the cosmos becomes more restrictive.

As Karl Löwith observes, the Greek was not concerned with man's distant future; his myths, genealogies, and histories represented their past as an ever present foundation.[5]

This is not to say that all forms of progress were foreign to the classical mind. A recent book, *The Idea of Progress in Classical*

---

[3] Cf. Edith Hamilton, *The Greek Way* (New York: New American Library, 1963), pp. 164–172.
[4] Mircea Eliade, *The Myth of the Eternal Return* (Princeton, N.J.: Princeton University Press, 1949), ix.
[5] Karl Löwith, *Meaning in History* (Chicago: University of Chicago Press, 1949), p. 221.

Antiquity, by the late Ludwig Edelstein challenges the traditional notion of progress in the ancient world. It is Dr. Edelstein's contention that a progressivist theory is to be found in classical thought, and that progressivism is latent even in ancient cyclic theory. He feels that Comte, Dilthey, and Bury were personally responsible for what he considers an unwarranted academic prejudice of considering ancient thought lacking a theory of progress.

> . . . I cannot persuade myself that one all-encompassing answer could ever describe adequately the attitude of a civilization that lasted for more than a millenium or that the forces of the progressivisms and anti-progressivisms were constants to be computed by adding and comparing bits of evidence as if they were numerals and as if the views embodied in them were independent of time and circumstance.[6]

Professor Manuel observes the general directions of development:

> If we follow these two shapes of philosophical history, the cyclical and the progressive. . . . they will reveal themselves to be less a logical than a psychological polarity. In any period there may be a weightier commitment to one or the other, but neither has ever dominated the European intellectual field without the presence in some form of its rival.[7]

[6] Ludwig Edelstein, *The Idea of Progress in Classical Antiquity* (Baltimore, Maryland: Johns Hopkins Press, 1967), p. xxvi. Compare this with Arnold Toynbee's observation: "The essential postulate is that in the successive or simultaneous careers of the various known civilizations—Egyptian and Mesopotamian and Minoan, Indian and Far Eastern, Hellenic and Syro-Iranian, Byzantine and Western and Middle Eastern—the historical vision reveals to us a profoundly significant and profoundly moving repetition of human experience on the heroic scale. When formulated in terms, this postulate may present the appearance of a somewhat formidable dogma; and yet, implicitly, it has surely always been the creed of every classical scholar." *Greek Historical Thought* (New York: Oxford University Press, 1952), p. xxiv. Robert Flint, on the other hand, says that the Greeks and Romans believed in history as a process of deterioration, progress, and cycle "although in none profoundly or consistently." *Philosophy of History* (New York: 1894), p. 90.

[7] Frank E. Manuel, *Shapes of Philosophical History* (Stanford, California, Stanford University Press, 1965), p. 5.

It may not be possible to pinpoint the origin of classical cyclicism. Hesiod, as early as the eighth century B.C. in his theory of
the five ages, gives some idea of patterned history. Hesiod tries
to find common ancestors among the many deities in his explanation of the world, a genealogical approach to the explanation
of the origin and development of the universe that was to
endure long after the Milesians abandoned mythology. The fact
that we are concerned with world origins and periodic recurrence of growth cycles need not obscure the fact that efforts were
also being made in such areas as medicine, astronomy, biology,
and mathematics as early as the sixth century B.C.

GREEK PHILOSOPHICAL THOUGHT AND HISTORY

The Ionians, Thales, Anaximander, and Anaximenes, were
particularly concerned with the problem of cosmogony, an understandable preoccupation of primitive man.[8] Anaximander's
theory of the eternal "Boundless" is particularly relevant to cyclic
thought, proposing as it did a primal substance giving rise to the
world's varied realities by a repetitious and endless process of
building up and tearing down.[9]

Heraclitus, the great philosopher of change, taught in the sixth
century B.C. that fire, the ultimate and quasi-spiritual substance
of nature, is the source from which the other elements of earth,
air, and water evolve, and to which they return in complete
cosmic cycles of formation and conflagration—variously identified

[8] The term primitive is not employed here in any technical anthropological
sense, but in the academician's ambiguous manner of describing his limited
knowledge rather than his subject's sophistication.

[9] Professor Grace Cairns (who has perhaps written the best single volume in
English on early cyclicism) observes: "Anaximenes' cyclical theory is similar except that he thinks the ultimate substance to be air instead of *Apeiron* (the
Boundless)." *Philosophies of History* (New York: 1962), p. 204. Chs. IX
and X, pp. 196–232 might well be read in their entirety; also G. S. Kirk
and J. E. Raven, *The Pre-Socratic Philosophers* (Cambridge: Cambridge University Press, 1960), Ch. I, "The Forerunners of Philosophical Cosmology,"
pp. 8–72.

as 18,000 years and 10,800 years.[10] The idiom is still primitive
and the sources limited, but a nascent scientific interest looms
in the mythopoeic description of the universe. Man's obligation,
according to Heraclitus, is to try to comprehend the underlying
wisdom of the world as expressed in the Logos, for human
behavior as well as physical nature is controlled by the Logos.
This Logos is the supreme ruler, not a personal God, but the
source of intelligence, energy, and life. "God is day-night, winter-
summer, war-peace, satiety-hunger." Universes come and go
everlastingly, but the Logos is.

Not only in prosperous Ionia, the crossroads of the ancient
world, where Greek philosophy and commerce both thrived, did
the systematic rationalistic effort to understand the physical
world take place. A second great stage in Pre-Socratic speculation
was that of the Italian Pythagorean schools. The Pythagoreans,
also in the sixth century B.C., viewing a world in which night
yielded to day, season to season, considered it reasonable to
assume that human experience (including successive re-incarna-
tions) was reflective of the rhythmic patterns of nature. "Their
cyclical view was founded on the astronomical idea of a Great
Year of the universe, a time at which all the heavenly bodies and
the earth would return to the same position." [11]

The religious orientation of the Pythagoreans reminds us that
both rite and myth are to primitive society what metaphysical
affirmation is to a later classical era, and both are geared to the
eternal and permanent, rather than to the fleeting and transitory.

[10] Cf. Arthur Lovejoy and George Boas, *Primitivism and Related Ideas in
Antiquity* (Baltimore: Johns Hopkins University Press, 1935), p. 79; and G. S.
Kirk and J. E. Raven, *op. cit.*, Ch. VI: "Heraclitus of Ephesus," pp. 182–215.
Professor Frederick Copleston, however, insists that the Stoics are responsible
for attributing the doctrine of periodic conflagration to Heraclitus. Cf. Frederick
Copleston, *A History of Philosophy* (New York: Doubleday, 1964), Vol. I,
pp. 44, 389.
[11] Grace E. Cairns, *op. cit.*, pp. 205–206. Cf. "The Pythagoreans and Eternal
Recurrence" in W. K. C. Guthrie, *History of Greek Philosophy* (Cambridge: Cambridge University Press, 1962), Vol. I, p. 281: "Once in being, the cosmos was
in all probability believed to be everlasting. We have no direct statement of the
fact, but Zeller was justified in inferring it from the doctrine of the exact repetition of history which is vouched for as Pythagorean by Eudemus. . . ."

Hesiod could look back in his own time, recall the ancient myths of the marriage of heaven and earth, and the birth of the gods, in a manner that would be alien to Democritus, the Atomist, a few centuries later. Admittedly, the forces of science are already gathering in the sixth century B.C. to replace mythology in the prestigious Ionian cities of Asia Minor. The myths of the gods are gradually detached from cosmogony, a new thought structure evolves, and by the fifth century B.C. authentically scientific questions are being asked.

Pythagoreanism was to enjoy, with Stoicism, a later vogue in Rome in the second and first centuries B.C., and the periodic renewal of the world was still an important theme.[12]

Of greater importance is the cyclic thought of Plato (428–348 B.C.), who pictures in the *Timaeus* a Great Cosmic Year in which the planets fulfill their respective rotations. The Demiurge, however, is the cause of the repetitive eternally patterned universe. In Greco-Oriental literature the Great Year is a sequence of creation and chaos, a fusion of the elements of degeneration and formation in such a way that eternal newness is preserved.

> Now everything that becomes or is created must of necessity be created by some cause, for without a cause nothing can be created. The work of the Creator, whenever he looks to the unchangeable and fashions the form and nature of his work after an unchangeable pattern must necessarily be made fair and perfect . . .[13]

The model of which the natural world is a copy is unchanging and eternal, but the copy in the sensible order is subject to a variation which precludes the possibility of exact scientific knowledge and requires progressive empirical investigation. And

[12] Mircea Eliade, *op. cit.*, pp. 122–123.
[13] *The Dialogues of Plato*, trans. B. Jowett, New York: 1937, I (28), p. 12. This is the one Platonic dialogue that deals with natural science and cosmogony, and, as A. E. Taylor says, "furnished the earlier Middle Ages with their standing general scheme of the natural world." *Plato, the Man and His Work* (London: 1952), p. 446. Cf. F. M. Cornford, *Plato's Cosmology* (London: 1937). This work is a translation and a commentary on the *Timaeus*.

although Plato did believe in cultural changes that were vaguely correlated with astronomical cycles, one cannot make a completely satisfactory case for recurrence theory in his thought.

For one thing, the *Timaeus* is a poetical statement of creation, and it is by no means obvious that Plato meant it to be taken literally. For another, the dynamism of the Platonic ethic and the importance of what Cornford has called "Socratic aspiration" in his thought would seem to suggest an emphasis on human freedom considerably at variance with cyclic determinism. Karl Popper, among others, has noted the presence of two contradictory tendencies in Plato's work: the thought of the man who plans by rational means to mould social and political institutions, and the thought of the determinist who recognizes in all things human a certain historical inevitability. A case might indeed be made for Plato's belief in a progressive decay that would resemble linearism rather than cyclicism; but there is little evidence of anything but a mythic view of philosophical pessimism. One must be content with seeing important cyclic elements in Plato's thought without seeing definitive presentation.

Connected to the complete revolution of the heavens is patterned behavior (ambiguously identified in Platonic thought at 10,000 years and 36,000 years), although Plato does not suggest an exact Pythagorean or Stoic sequence and conformity of events and personalities (*Republic*, VIII, 546).

The *Republic* (of which the *Timaeus* is a continuation), *Critias*, and the *Statesman* all consider the culture cycle and the correlation of human culture with the astronomical rotations of the heavenly spheres.[14] At least in a general way, cultural experience reflects astronomical change in which a rhythmic rise and fall measures out historical existence. Destruction ensues

[14] Cf. especially Plato's description of God's relation, estrangement, and renewed relation with his world in the *Statesman*, 270–274, and the discussion of cyclic number in the *Republic*, 546. For a treatment of the subject in general, see W. H. Walsh, "Plato and the Philosophy of History," *History and Theory*, II, 1 pp. 3–16.

from man's periodic avarice, lust for power, and hatred of wisdom.[15]

Plato, therefore, despite the fact that he seems to be influenced to some degree by the astral thought of the Chaldeans, never believed, apparently, in rigid repetition of historical events.

Aristotle himself was critical of the creationist theory he professed to find in the *Timaeus*, but it would seem more probable that Plato did not mean to assert the existence of a *time* before the construction of the world, but represents the world as having a beginning (as the Neoplatonists maintain) for explanatory purposes only.[16]

Aristotle's belief in prime movers in no sense means his acceptance of creationism in any form. He considers the world to be eternal and subject to periodic recurrence in the generation and corruption of organic types and in the recurrence of cultural patterns. Coming-to-be and passing-away are processes always occurring in nature, their repetitive character being accounted for by the nature of matter itself.[17] God, the eternally self-conscious thought, elicits as the final, but not efficient cause, the motion of the concentric spheres of the heavens.

In Aristotle's peculiar interplay of metaphysical and astronomical elements, all realities are recognized as having an allotted span of development, maturation, and decay, although in Aristotle too the repetitive form of existence does not extend to the

---

[15] Cf. Grace E. Cairns, *op. cit.*, p. 216.

[16] Cf. A. E. Taylor, *op. cit.*, pp. 442–443. A. H. Armstrong says: ". . . Though there was much dispute among the ancient Platonists on this point, it seems fairly clear that Plato did not intend his description of the Craftsman to be taken literally to the point of asserting a beginning of the world in time. He is giving us a cosmology in the time-honored mythical form of a cosmogony, showing what he regards as the essential elements in the universe, by telling a symbolical story of its making." *An Introduction to Ancient Philosophy* (Westminster, Md.: The Newman Press, 1957), pp. 48–49. Cf. also Richard McKeon, *The Basic Works of Aristotle* (New York: Random House, 1941); *Physics*, Book VIII, Ch. 1–8 (250b–265a), pp. 354–387; *On the Heavens*, Book I, Ch. 10–12 279b–292b), pp. 419–428; *Metaphysics*, Book XII, Ch. 6–7 (1071b–1073a), pp. 877–881.

[17] Aristotle, *On Generation and Corruption*, Book I, Ch. 3 (317b–319b), McKeon ed., pp. 478–484.

exact reproduction of previous historical experience in its minutiae.

Cyclicism not only extends to nature but to the social and political creations of man. The human institution begins hesitantly, grows, waxes strong, and decays. Social forms have their models in the cosmic pattern. "The state of beatitude itself, *eudaimonia*, is an imitation of the divine condition, not to mention the various kinds of *enthousiasmos* created in the soul of man by the repetition of certain acts realized by the gods . . ."[18] Man's very happiness is spelled out in paradigmatic acts imitative of a basically contemplative God.[19]

Zeno, the founder of the Stoic school, was born in the fourth century B.C. and lived most of his life in Athens. After an early interest in Cynicism, he established his own school about the year 300 B.C. Of his followers, Cleanthes and Chryssipus are perhaps the best known.

The Stoics in their philosophy of nature were indebted to both Heraclitus and the Pythagoreans. Fire is the essential world stuff, although it assumes a dualistic form in which the passive element is matter and the active element God. God, though possessed of consciousness, is material—a primal fire from which all goes forth and to which all returns in an unending series of formation and destruction.[20]

Moreover, the Stoic form is the most rigid of recurrence theories, positing as it does an exact sequence of identical worlds in which both nature and men follow identically repetitive patterns. Chryssipus is to say that there will come again and again a Socrates, a Plato, the same friends in the same situations. Fate, of course, supersedes any meaningful freedom and is identical with God and universal reason; man can only alter

[18] Mircea Eliade, *op. cit.*, p. 32.
[19] Aristotle, *Nicomachean Ethics* (1178b), McKeon ed., pp. 1106–1107.
[20] Cf. P. Merlan, Ch. VII, "The Stoa," in *The Cambridge History of Later Greek and Early Medieval Philosophy* (London–New York: Cambridge University Press, 1967), pp. 124–132. The thought of the early, middle, and late Stoa is markedly different. Merlan sees ambiguity in a monistic determinism that would leave a significant place for prescriptive ethics. Posidonius is particularly important in this early period of Stoic cosmology.

his reaction to events rather than choose or alter the events themselves. Later Stoic philosophers like Seneca, Epictetus, and Marcus Aurelius modify both the determinism and the materialism of the early Stoa, but Marcus Aurelius considers the soul as taken up once again after the world conflagration; and somber Seneca had his own version of cyclic destruction and rebirth.[21]

The Epicureans, though roughly contemporaneous with the Stoics, had a more materialistically oriented theory of periodic recurrence that is of special interest because of its modern revival in the thought of Nietzsche. Since the universe is composed of limited kinds of atomic particles (as described by Democritus), all possibilities will not only be realized, but will inevitably recur, granted an infinity of duration. Epicurus does not accept the Stoic theory of exact temporal sequence or the bizarre theory of the reproduction of similar historical personalities.

Nothing proceeds from nothing, and nothing passes into nothingness. The atoms assume different configuration in the timeless void, recede into an atomic pool, and historically reappear.

This brief account of cyclicism in the thought of Hesiod, the Milesians, Heraclitus, Plato, Aristotle, the Pythagoreans, Stoics, and Epicureans is indicative of a distinctly classical way of looking at the historical experience that resembles nothing that is familiar to us today. As Eliade observes, it is not merely that sacred and profane time are different, but that the experience of time as such is not the same for primitive and western man.

The classical way of looking at reality excludes both religious creationism and linear progressivism. It is a vision of time which rejects the unique linear event as unworthy of historical notice because it does not conform to the meaningful archetypes.

The ancient's use of myth, rite, and symbol constitute the expression of this way of life and a rejection of the theory of profane time. Rite and sacrifice go back to a remembered and

[21] Grace E. Cairns, op. cit., pp. 220–222. The Stoa strongly emphasize a cosmic religiousness. Plotinus especially pleads for a freedom of the will that is not easily reconcilable with the thought of Stoicism in general. Cf. Merlan, op. cit., p. 130.

recreated event that is not lost in the passing of the years; its very sameness resists the erosion of time and suggests a permanent and enduring transcendent reality. But when religious sensitivity fades, repetition takes on more pessimistic overtones.[22]

The symbol is significant because its very meaning is derived from repetitive association. If the ego and thing have but an isolated encounter, the language of symbol could not exist.

The Homeric myth itself may represent a comparatively unsophisticated and unscientific approach to reality, but it too protests against passing time by appealing to the metatemporal gods, who may be capricious, promiscuous, or unpleasant, but never mortal.[23] Toynbee suggests that Hellenic historical thought began when Homeric poetry shaped itself in the Greek mind.

The Greek's historical outlook was not disinterest in the future as much as an existential affirmation of permanence, and a belief in teleology, however dimly seen.

When contemporary theologians like Rahner, Richard, Robinson, Schillebeeckx, and Cox remind us that the secular is not a realm distinct from the sacred, it is interesting to reflect that the ancient world gave sacred meaning to such profane meaningful activities as hunting, fishing, farming, playing, and loving. Mircea Eliade notes:

> If we observe the general behavior of archaic man, we are struck by the following fact: neither the objects of the external world nor human acts, properly speaking, have any autonomous intrinsic value. Objects or acts acquire a value, and in so doing become real, because they participate, after one fashion or another, in a reality that transcends them.[24]

[22] For an analogical study of the religious and historical significance of sacred and profane space, cf. Mircea Eliade, *The Sacred and the Profane* (New York: Harper and Row, 1961), Ch. II, "Sacred Space and Making the World Sacred," pp. 68–115.

[23] R. A. F. MacKenzie observes: "Myth is always an attempt to express, and thereby to make comprehensible, some truth about the world and man's existence in it, a truth inaccessible and unknown in itself, but capable of being expressed in and by symbols." *Faith and History in the Old Testament* (New York: Macmillan, 1966), p. 71.

[24] Mircea Eliade, *The Myth of the Eternal Return*, pp. 3–4. On the remoteness of God, see Eliade's *The Sacred and the Profane*, pp. 121–125; and Rudolf Otto, *The Idea of the Holy* (New York: Harper, 1958), pp. 5–30.

As has been suggested, what to the modern is a frustrating confinement within fate's circle was to the ancient a quest for the static and permanent, a sharing in a primordial and transcendent unity in such a way that every meaningful secular act has its sacred counterpart. The fact that such an act would recur again was not a depressing sign of mythic tyranny but a sign that the individual in his being as well as in his activity was a part of a teleological whole.

The Homeric poetry and cosmogony which characterized the greatness of Ionian culture were both reflective of a concern for archetypal permanence. The stories of the gods and the eternally recurring universe were twin ways of myth and science by which the ancient rejected the concrete historical time of Ionian history. And when the great age of Athenian culture appeared, the theme of eternal recurrence, though formulated with more sophistication, remained as a basic historical outlook.

Perfection is represented by the circle, which assures repetition of essential and permanent realities; consequently all cosmic becoming is subject to immutable law. What has been, will be. Another Pythagoras will teach at Croton. Another Parmenides will say:

> God is equal in all directions to himself,
> Altogether eternal,
> A rounded sphere enjoying circular solitude.

Another Socrates will drink hemlock and another Plato will teach at another Academy in another Athens. No happening is unique and inexplicable, for then it would be meaningless. Historical existence is repetition and recurrence.[25]

It should be added that cyclic thought is by no means limited to the Greco-Roman world, although the Greco-Roman world has been the focal point of our interest. It is found in the ancient cultures of Mesopotamia and Egypt, where it was based on the

[25] Cf. J. B. Bury, *The Greek Historians* (New York: Random House, 1958), pp. 205–207.

observation of the heavens, and human and animal experiences of life and death, space, and time.

> Man the thinker and inventor of hypotheses . . . developed philosophical ideas of cosmic cycles which became the typical view of history in the great civilizations of India and Greece; also in China, this notion is found in a unique and indigenous form.[26]

For instance, in Hinduism and in the Buddhism that developed from it, the world cycle of destruction and renovation is a common theme. But it is the wheel rather than the circle which symbolizes the historical in Oriental thought. In the Jainist tradition the wheel of time moves inexorably onward in the revolving rhythm of the Avasarpini and Utsarpini ages, and the individual's aim is not to escape from the circular into linear and profane time, but to become a part of the eternal.[27]

Whether it be geometrically symbolized in a Mahayana Buddhism's *Mandala* or the Hindu *Yantra*, recurrence in both cosmic and psychological realms is very much a part of the Oriental philosophy which stresses man's vital involvement with nature.

It will be seen how cyclic thought has more than historical significance, not only in the revival of Epicurean cyclicism in the thought of Nietzsche and the morphological determinism of Spengler, but in the medieval thought of Siger of Brabant and Dante, and in the later philosophy of Schelling.[28] In a qualified way it will be combined with linearism in the thought of Sorokin.

SUGGESTED READINGS

I. THE GREEK AND HIS WORLD

A. H. Armstrong, *An Introduction to Ancient Philosophy*, Westminster, Maryland: The Newman Press, 1957, pp. 1–8.

---

[26] Grace E. Cairns, *op. cit.*, xvi.

[27] Cf. Sir Charles Eliot, *Hinduism and Buddhism* (New York: Barnes and Noble, 1921), Vol. I, pp. 42–47.

[28] Karl Löwith, *op. cit.*, p. 257. Löwith also cites a combination of cyclical and Christian world views in the prologue of Goethe's *Faust*.

Harry Elmer Barnes, *A History of Historical Writing, New York: Dover, 1962, pp. 26–40.

C. M. Bowra, *The Greek Experience, New York: New American Library, 1957, pp. 32–53, 97–114.

F. M. Cornford, *Before and After Socrates, London: Cambridge University Press, 1960, pp. 1–28.

Kathleen Freeman, God, Man and State: Greek Concepts, London: McDonald & Co., 1952.

W. K. C. Guthrie, *The Greeks and Their Gods, Boston: Beacon, 1955, Ch. X, "Hopes and Fears of the Ordinary Man," pp. 254–309.

Edith Hamilton, *The Greek Way, New York: New American Library, 1963.

Werner Jaeger, Paideia, The Ideals of Greek Culture, New York: Oxford University Press, 1945, I, pp. 3–14.

G. S. Kirk and J. E. Raven, *The Pre-Socratic Philosophers, London: Cambridge University Press, 1960, pp. 1–72.

Alfred Zimmern, The Greek Commonwealth, New York: Oxford University Press, 1956, Part II, Politics, pp. 51–214.

II. ETERNAL RECURRENCE IN WESTERN THOUGHT

Grace E. Cairns, *Philosophies of History, New York: 1962, Chs. IX–X, pp. 196–232.

R. G. Collingwood, Essays in the Philosophy of History, Austin, Texas: University of Texas, 1965, Ch. V, "The Theory of Historical Cycles," pp. 76–89.

Ludwig Edelstein, The Idea of Progress in Classical Antiquity, Baltimore: Johns Hopkins University Press, 1967, pp. xi–xxxiii, 21–56.

Mircea Eliade, *The Myth of the Eternal Return, Princeton, N.J.: Princeton University Press, 1949, pp. 112–138; *The Sacred and the Profane, New York: Harper and Row, 1961, pp. 109–113; Patterns in Comparative Religion, New York: Meridian, 1963, Ch. XI, "Sacred Time and the Myth of Eternal Renewal," pp. 388–409.

David Greene, *Greek Political Theory, Chicago: University of Chicago Press, 1965, Ch. VIII, "Beyond Necessity," pp. 80–92.

Karl Löwith, Meaning in History, Chicago: University of Chicago Press, 1946, pp. 214–222.

Frank E. Manuel, Shapes of Philosophical History, Stanford: Stanford University Press, 1965, pp. 1–23.

Arnold Toynbee, Greek Historical Thought, New York: New American Library, 1952, pp. ix–xxv.

Perhaps the best single English language reference source in Greek philosophy is the not-yet-completed work, A History of Greek Philosophy by W. K. C. Guthrie, Cambridge: Cambridge University Press, Vol. I, 1962, Vol. II, 1965. Five volumes are planned to cover the whole period of ancient Greek philosophy, the most comprehensive effort in English since the translated work of Theodore Comperz in 1909.

CHAPTER THREE

ST. AUGUSTINE AND LINEAR HISTORY

When the great Augustine began writing *The City of God* he was not particularly concerned about writing a treatise on historical interpretation. That his *City of God* became the great literary embodiment of Christian linearism was a development probably unforeseen by Augustine who was quite concerned about the immediate practical problems of supposed Christian responsibility for the sack of Rome in A.D. 410. He was quite aware of the pagan charge that the diminution of Roman power and prestige was to be attributed to Christian animosity to the gods of Rome. He writes first as a Christian apologist, and second as a social and political theorist who saw two diametrically opposed loves building antithetical ways of life. Augustine is not an urban planner; his "city" is but the symbol of an entire philosophy of life which either accepts or rejects the primacy of love of God and neighbor over selfish and materially-oriented interest. Augustine's world is stratified into spiritual and corporeal levels, and his monumental if diffuse excursion into the realms of public and private morality is a continuation of a fundamental outlook developed in earlier works.[1]

[1] Cf. especially *The First Catechetical Instruction*, trans. by J. P. Christopher, *Ancient Christian Writers Series* (Westminster, Maryland: The Newman Press, 1946), Vol. II.

Augustine is aware of the materialistic heritage of so much of Greek philosophy which reacted so early against the myths of Homer and Hesiod. He sees in Plotinus and Plato an attempt to salvage spiritual values endangered by the Epicurean and Stoic traditions. And he is aware that the faith has to find a meaningful philosophic or rational idiom if it is to communicate meaningfully to its time.

As an apologist he employs a forthright and at times an unnecessarily combative style. He ridicules the recurrence theory (the *circuitus temporum* he labels it) as an argumentation of infidels who wish to drag the faithful from the straight road "to walk on the wheel." That events should endlessly recur was offensive to his Christian sensibilities, which accepted a creation, the fall of man, a redemption, and a final *parousia* or second coming of Christ that would mark the end of the historical process itself. Augustine sees cyclicism not only as negating an essentially progressive salvation history but as an outlook that denied the meaning of freedom and the unique historical event in human history. The classical ideal cited by Mircea Eliade of an act's being meaningful precisely because it is repetitive and imitative of a recurring transcendent ontological model is utterly alien to Augustine's mind.

> Far be it from the true faith that we should believe that there are cycles in which similar revolutions of times and of temporal things are repeated so that, as one might say, just as in this age the philosopher Plato sat in the city of Athens and in a school called the Academy teaching his pupils, so also through countless ages of the past. . . . the same Plato and the same city and the same school and the same pupils have been repeated as they are destined to be repeated through countless ages of the future. God forbid that we should accept such nonsense! Christ died, once and for all, for our sins.[2]

Augustine, in accepting Christianity, accepts a vision of history that sees man advancing to an ultimate end, and while admitting

---

[2] *The City of God*, XII, 14, 21. St. Augustine's works are in Migne, *Patrologia Latina*, vols. 22 to 47. The 1945 Everyman edition of *The City of God* (London) is easily available.

that a common nature may act in a uniform and repetitive fashion, he is vehement in rejecting the notion that such repetition is inevitable. Both the individual and his wider freedom receive new emphasis. The future may not offer the comfortable circular security of a road that has been traveled before, but it does hold mystery and adventure, and the historical dimension and significance of an individual's acts are enormously heightened.

This is not to say that Augustine considers man's freedom as negating or even determining the over-all providential plan of God; but for Augustine man's authentic freedom is a part of that very providence. Professor Cochrane says:

> Augustine thus discovers the clue to human history, not in any fine spun philosophic abstraction (particles of matter ceaselessly grouping and regrouping themselves; the type monotonously repeating itself in countless individuals); but purely and simply in the congenital impulse of human beings to attain happiness.[3]

For Augustine the human situation is both glory and tragedy; glory because man, made to the image and likeness of God, may win the eternal beatitude that lies beyond the end of history, and tragedy because man may use his awesome freedom to turn away from God and destroy the purpose for which he was made.

Original sin has so flawed man's nature that one can assume neither clarity of vision nor rectitude of choice. Augustine sees the human dilemma in the language of a Paul lamenting the fact that he does the evil he wills not and avoids doing the good that he wills.

He places a great emphasis on individual human responsibility. Man must yield neither to a supposititious external destiny which supposedly controls him, nor to the internal solicitations of the flesh which tempts him. But he remains free to be a member of the society of saints or sinners as he chooses. His love will take him to one of two cities.

[3] Charles Norris Cochrane, *Christianity and Classical Culture* (Oxford: Oxford University Press, 1959), p. 486.

That which animates the secular society is the love of self to the point of contempt for God. That which animates divine society is love of God to the point of contempt for self.[4]

There is not only an eschatological dimension to Augustine's thought but a definite political and social one. Recurrence theory as exemplified in the third book of Plato's *Laws*, for instance, concerned itself not only with cycles of nature, but with definite political cycles in which states would come into existence and die at intervals. Polybius in *The Histories* considers the periodic rise and fall of states, empires, and even constitutions as dictated by nature, and it is perhaps in its political rather than in its astronomical or psychological form that cyclicism survived the longest in the medieval and Renaissance worlds.

To Thucydides, as to Polybius, history's significance was found in the repetition of human experience; to Augustine, neither freedom nor history can be meaningful unless under the providence of God human experience is individual and unique.

Augustine, of course, articulated an already existing Christian tradition that had more than three centuries to develop before his birth in 354 A.D.

The first century Jewish philosopher, Philo of Alexandria, had seen the dilemma that existed in reconciling biblical linearism and cyclical recurrence; and even the great Origen, in the third century, despite his great sympathy for the classical outlook, saw folly in a Platonic cyclicism which suggests that "another Socrates will be born who will marry another Xanthippe." [5] He does seem, however, to be torn between a modified cyclicism which Dawson sees as resembling the Hindu *samsara*—the endless chain of existence—and the theory of irreversible time that is biblical.

Clement of Rome, writing to the Church at Corinth in the second century, sees history as a school by which men may be instructed in righteousness by the example of successive generations.

[4] *The City of God*, XIV, 28.
[5] *Against Celsus*, IV, 68.

A half century later, the apologist Justin Martyr will view history in terms of divine fulfillment, showing a remarkable sophistication in his appreciation of pagan scholarship and secular achievement.

But it is in the work of Irenaeus of Lyons at the end of the second century that the linear tradition and apostolic succession are emphasized strongly along with chronology. The first detailed chronology is put together by Julius Africanus early in the third century, a work that was significant not in settling a dispute between Tatian and Clement of Alexandria about the dates of Moses, but because it attempted to relate sacred events with contemporaneous secular history.[6]

Another transitional figure like Tertullian, still influenced by the classical tradition, looks to nature to prove a theory of progressivistic change, utilizes Stoic language to describe the soul, and recognizes the inevitability of a materialistic millennium— yet is trying to free himself from a cyclical outlook obviously at variance with his severe Montanist conscience.

The Fathers of the Church, Eusebius, Justin Martyr, Gregory of Nyssa also wrote of the incompatibility of recurrence theory with the unique linear historicity of the creation, incarnation, and judgment as contained in Christian revelation.

Professor Manuel observes:

> The sacred generations, taught the Fathers, succeeded one another, every womb bearing novelty. There was a great beginning and thereafter ever new beginnings until the final end. If there was an apparent similarity between one set of historical events and a succeeding one, the former was to be understood as a prefiguration. Babylon pre-figured Rome, David the Christ, the ark the Church. This idea of prefiguration, so crucial for Christian history, soon became a felicitous way of unconsciously assimilating the historical cyclism of pagan thought without injuring the truth of directed Christian movement.
>
> The patristic rejection of Greek and Roman cyclism doubtless had many antecedents in post-exilic Judaism, and there are those

---

[6] R. L. P. Milburn, *Early Christian Interpretations of History* (New York: Hillary, 1954), p. 35.

who trace its origins even further back to Zoroastrianism. Be that as it may, from the age of the Apostles on, no Christian could believe in the new man of St. Paul who supersedes the old Adam and at the same time tolerate Stoic cyclical conceptions.[7]

To understand Augustine is to understand not only his inheritance from the earlier Fathers, but also his dependence on a Jewish historical tradition of many centuries. To Augustine "the task of history is to record events faithfully and in a serviceable manner." [8] But the great African has had a chance to get used to not only a distinctively Christian outlook, but an outlook which was not in its origin distinctively different from the Jewish tradition from which it emerged. As Rabbi Solomon Goldman phrases it, "Inspired authors wrote history instead of a theology or philosophy, and dramatized the destiny of all people in the career of a people." [9]

THE JEWS AND HISTORY

The Hebrews had an essentially simple approach to the problem of history. Yahweh is the one God who guides the destinies of men and nations in a purposive and meaningful direction. There is a fundamental unity in historical experience. "Israel's credo is presented as a revelation from God that occurred at specific times in specific places to identifiable men." [10]

Civilization is a cooperative venture of God and man working against the discordant element of evil which early enters the scene. God makes a covenant with his people, and despite their

---

[7] Frank E. Manuel, *Shapes of Philosophical History* (Stanford, California: Stanford University Press, 1965), p. 13.

[8] *De doctrina Christiana*, II, 28.

[9] Solomon Goldman, *The Book of Books: An Introduction* (New York: Harper, 1948), p. 10.

[10] R. A. F. MacKenzie, *Faith and History in the Old Testament* (New York: Macmillan, 1966), p. 69. Cf. also Rudolf Bultmann, *History and Eschatology* (New York: Charles Scribner's Sons, 1962), Ch. II, "The Understanding of History in the Era before Christ," pp. 12–22.

many inadequacies and infidelities, he remains their God and they remain his people.

> At crucial moments he had rendered special assistance. He saved Noah from destruction by the flood; he called Abraham to become the ancestor of a chosen people; he summoned Moses to deliver the Israelites from their bondage in Egypt; he established the nation under David in Palestine; he led the faithful back from their exile in Babylonia; he rescued the people from threatened destruction by the Syrian kings; and he would ultimately establish the Jewish nation triumphantly in the Holy Land when all other kingdoms would be either annihilated or converted to the Jewish faith.[11]

The Jewish historical experience was indeed replete with frustration · and defeat, but the essential confidence in God who would eventually make all things right was never destroyed. The forces of Syria, Egypt, Persia, Mesopotamia, and Rome would batter the chosen people, but Jewish hope would survive. What was fostered by successive invasion was a messianic nationalism that placed a perhaps disproportionate emphasis on political stability and national identity that was considered then as now necessary for survival in an alien world.

The restoration of a militarily powerful Davidic kingdom was only one of the hopes of ancient Israel. More significant perhaps was the expectation of a divine intervention in which a chosen one of God would sustain the political and religious hopes of Israel and confirm to the world their role as a vehicle of divine purpose. Adversaries would be destroyed by the same kind of extraordinary intervention in the historical process that was reflected in the Flood or the covenant with Abraham.

A piquant quality of melancholy and expectation suggests the Jewish mentality. The almost perpetual harassment of the chosen people made them long for the certainty and stability of former ages, but the mood was ambivalent in that expectation

---

[11] Shirley Jackson Case, *The Christian Philosophy of History* (Chicago: University of Chicago Press, 1943), pp. 16–17.

of a future fulfillment was also a part of the vision. Jewish history tended to be the past as remembered rather than the past "as it actually happened." Genesis, for instance, conveys great themes, not in terms of academic precision that would satisfy the contemporary critical historian, but in non-technical terms that suggest an earlier oral tradition of considerable duration.[12]

The Hebrew, like the ancient Greek, not only worshipped his God, but saw in temple ritual the means of capturing the timeless values of an ancient faith in a passing and largely hostile world of ephemeral values. Rabbinic additions to sacred scripture provided a more specific and static tradition in almost all sectors of private and public life. But nowhere do we find a sympathy for cyclicism in the classic sense.

In contemporaneous civilizations we find some interesting contrasts. Egyptian documents attesting to military exploits, economic, legal, and administrative affairs reveal a concept of history that testifies to a static condition rather than progressivistic development.[13] And in nearby Mesopotamia the situation is similar. The belief in static gods and awe of nature precluded the possibility of looking at history as meaningful process.

The Hebrews looked to a temporal consummation of the historical process, but they were not intimidated by profane time as their imprecise chronologies reveal. Their interest is in the story and its message, not in its minutiae. And the scribes, the priests, and the prophets whose task it was to commit the oral tradition to writing (and upon whose work our vision of Hebrew history principally rests) reflect this interest in the grander concerns of man's destiny. When McKenzie says that the Hebrews did not see God in history, but history in God, he recognizes the fact that the secular and sacred experience are not greatly separated.[14] Yahweh inaugurates all and is in all, not as a constitutive

---

[12] John McKenzie, *The Two-Edged Sword* (New York: Doubleday, 1967), p. 87.
[13] Ludlow Bull, "Ancient Egypt," in The Idea of History in the Ancient Near East, ed. Robert Penton (New Haven: Yale University Press, 1955), p. 32.
[14] John McKenzie, op. cit., p. 93.

pantheistic principle, but as one actually involved in the vast secular integument called history.

Early Hebrew chronology was based on the computing of time by generations of about forty years duration, and on the pivotal event of the Fall of Man. Historical chronicle develops in the great reigns of David and Solomon, and there is an amazing sophistication to be found in Hebrew historical narrative. Barnes notes the comparative sophistication of Hebrew history when Egyptian, Babylonian, and Assyrian contemporaries were still preoccupied with dull chronicle, the wars of kings, and the tales of folk heroes.

Professor Barnes adds:

> The Books of Kings were the first practical illustration of the notion of history as "philosophy teaching by example." The author sought primarily to convince his people of the value of religious fidelity by citing historical illustrations of the disasters that had come to the Hebrews because they deserted their national religion. The author of Kings, in the synchronous history of Israel and Judah and the story of the later Judean kings, drew upon valuable early records whose factual accuracy has, in the main, often been corroborated by contemporary inscriptions. The chronicles are distinctly inferior in accuracy.[15]

The Old Testament remains a remarkable presentation of a national tradition recorded by an anguished and persecuted people.

Hebrew history is not merely guided by God; it is a record of his acts and his extraordinary interventions in the historical process. It is paradoxically explanatory and esoteric: explanatory in that it is a recitation of the *gesta Dei* themselves; esoteric in that awe and reverence for God's transcendence prevent not only symbolic artistic representation of his person, but by the third century B.C. an avoidance of the very mention of the name Yahweh in favor of the less sacred forms of Adonai and Elohim.

The linear character of the history that Augustine was to write

---

[15] Harry Elmer Barnes, A *History of Historical Writing* (New York: Dover, 1962), p. 23.

was shaped largely by the messianic element of the Jewish outlook, whether it took the form of a primarily political Davidic messiahship or a more spiritually oriented messiahship foretold by the prophets.

The coming of this messiah—the apocalyptic event as Collingwood would label it—would be the pivotal historical event, the eschaton, considered not as the end of history, but as its turning point.[16]

The advent of the messiah as foreshadowed in Jewish history, or as realized in Christian, presumes linear development. One may construe this linearism as spiral in character inasmuch as there is both progression and a kind of repetition in historical experience. But the great landmarks of Jewish history are clearly delineated—(the salvation story that Oscar Cullmann calls the *Heilsplan*), and these key events are not destined to be repeated. Man is created; he falls. Out of fallen humanity God chooses a special people for the salvation of mankind. And out of this people a "remnant of Israel," the *qehal Jahweh*. Cullmann sees this remnant as further reduced to the "Servant of Yahweh" referred to in Isaiah II and the "Son of Man" in Daniel. This person enters history as God, who, in rising, is triumphant over death. The reductive process from the people leads to the single person of Christ the Redeemer at the center of salvation history. And in the reversal of the process the multiple communities come into existence developing from the One. The church, the people of God, constitute the new remnant, the *ecclesia*.

Thus salvation history is seen as a development from the Many to the One in the Old Covenant and from the One to the Many in the New. Christ is not only to come at the end of history; he is established in its center.[17]

It is also significant that we find clues to the Jewish concept of history outside Sacred Scripture itself in related apocalyptic

---

[16] Karl Löwith, *Meaning in History* (Chicago: University of Chicago Press, 1949), p. 182.

[17] Cf. Oscar Cullmann, *Christ and Time* (Philadelphia: Westminster, 1964), pp. 116–118; and R. G. Collingwood, *The Idea of History* (Oxford: Oxford University Press, 1946), p. 50.

and Talmudic writings which represent not only scriptural commentary but a mass of rabbinical elaborations of an earlier oral
tradition largely codified by the sixth century A.D.

It would be erroneous to suppose that Christianity burst upon
the ancient world and created immediately a new historical consciousness. First of all, as has been mentioned, there was no truly
great historian in the first few centuries to record early Christian
development; and second, the Greco-Roman world was openly
contemptuous of both Christians and Jews, and considered it
preposterous that any such sects would assume for themselves
cosmic significance. Shotwell compares the classical attitude to
the Jews and early Christians to the lack of interest we have for
the beliefs of foreign immigrants settled in our city slums.[18]

It is also true that early Christian preoccupations were theological rather than political, a posture aided somewhat by a pre-
mature expectation of the Second Coming of Christ that suggested aloofness from the world and its concerns. Millennial
expectation is not conducive to secular scholarship, nor preoccupation with the secular order in general. The early Christian
did not formally cultivate an unhistorical attitude, but his primary concern was a God who lived above and beyond historical
time, and an eternal happiness that was outside the historian's
range of thought and effort.

The Judeo-Christian outlook was concerned with one question
of enormous historical importance: the validity of Christianity's
claim that Jewish expectation was realized in the person of
Christ. And patristic literature is intent on justifying Christ as
Messiah.

The unity that a Herodotus, Polybius, and Thucydides give to
isolated stories in the ancient world is, in a sense, matched by the
Christian conviction that God is the creator of a teleological
universe. But even in the absence of any towering historical
writers as such in the patristic period, the eschatological faith
that human experience had an ultimate meaning was a firm part

---

[18] J. T. Shotwell, *The History of History* (New York: Columbia University
Press, 1939), p. 279.

of the Christian belief. But it was a part of the belief of a community that began to realize that the Second Coming was not imminent, and a community that had with the edict of Constantine in A.D. 313 achieved considerable recognition before the law.

AUGUSTINE'S PHILOSOPHY OF HISTORY

The Augustine who writes the *City of God* is a disturbed man, a man who has seen Rome sacked by the Goths and who was to see at the end of his life Vandals at the gates of Hippo. Christianity "had arrived" to a position of respectability and responsibility by Augustine's time, but the political shell of the empire which encased it was cracking.

But Augustine's faith is not based on a contemplative aloofness from the temporal. History is a meaningful progression to an end, even when it brings periodic crucifixion. For Augustine the historical is a vital dimension of the salvation story itself. He is not concerned with the egocentricity of a Vergilian theology that would equate history with the fortunes of Rome, any more than he is sympathetic to traditional cyclicism.

Specifically, Augustine in the *City of God* is "one of the great bridges between classical antiquity and the modern world." [19] But although he is a neo-Platonist, he writes primarily as a Christian bishop and apologist, extolling "that most glorious society and celestial city of God's faithful." Professor Versfeld notes rather interestingly the resemblances between the *Republic* and *Laws* of Plato and the *City of God*. He notes Plato's concern for the rending of Greece in the Peloponnesian War and the necessity of justice and righteousness in social and political life. But the city of Plato's just man did not exist except in a rationalist dream, and events are related to permanent archetypes.

Augustine is dealing with an existent historical community

[19] Marthinus Versfeld, A *Guide to the City of God* (New York: Humanities Press, 1958), p. 1.

built upon actions which are unique in quality and linear in direction. Professor Shinn sees Augustine holding a thread composed of three strands.

> The first is the emphasis upon the ultimate eschatological fulfillment which gives meaning to an otherwise chaotic and incomplete history. The second is the significance within history of the divine society conceived as the true Church, in contrast to the earthly society. The third is the appreciation of history itself, including "secular" history and its dynamic possibilities of human achievement.[20]

If Augustine was disturbed by the capture of Rome by the Goths in A.D. 410, he was even more disturbed by the accusation of pagans in officially Christian Rome that such a calamity would not have occurred had Rome been faithful to her pagan gods.

His effort is to show the fragile character of any earthly enterprise and the particular vulnerability of an empire that was crumbling because of widespread immorality and irreligion. The empire which had its origins in the Greek city-state showed a remarkable degree of material sophistication and a persistent classical disdain for the moral values of the new faith. Not only did materialism hold sway in Carthage and Rome, but in the provinces as well. Secular materialistic values were the dominant values of the dying empire. Christopher Dawson observes:

> The one exception to this tendency is to be found in the Jewish tradition, and this was the one religious tradition which had preserved its independence in the face of the cosmopolitan Hellenistic culture. The attempt of the Seleucid kings to Hellenize Judea had led to the great national rising of the Maccabean period, which was nothing less than a crusade against Hellenism.[21]

The opposition between Christianity and imperial culture is complicated by the fact that the Church became a rallying point

---

[20] Roger L. Shinn, *Christianity, and the Problem of History* (New York: Bethany Press, 1963), pp. 52–53.

[21] Christopher Dawson, *A Monument to St. Augustine* (London: Sheed and Ward, 1945), Ch. I, "The Dying World," p. 23.

for the poor, the dissident, and those disenchanted with materialism; and as these elements attached themselves to a Church that was irrevocably committed to denying the pretensions of the emperor, open conflict became not probable but inevitable. An empire built on systematic exploitation of men and resources for the benefit of a privileged class could not hope to survive the political and social revolution that began as early as the second century.

It is to be noted, too, as Dawson maintains, that a theoretical harmony should have been obtained between Church and empire in order that both the spiritual and political unity of the human family might be achieved by corporate effort. But although the Church was to assume the authority structures of empire and retain its bureaucratic ways long after the empire had died, the goal of the universal society—Orosius' *Romania*— never did come into being, both because of the hostility of the old guard Romans who treasured Rome's gods as inseparable from her traditions, and the unconsolidated nature of Christianity herself.

The first ten books of the *City of God* concern themselves with the basic contention that the pagan gods are not to be worshipped for advantages in this life or the next. Augustine ridicules the idea that Christianity was the cause of the sack of Rome, citing in detail the inability of the pagan gods to avert the many calamities which befell Rome in earlier days. His unkindest cut of all is the suggestion that if the gods had an empire to give, it would have been to Greece.

He contrasts the crudity of Varro's "select" gods with the nobility of Christian belief, and asserts that Christ rather than *daemones*, good or bad, is the true mediator.

The epic of the two cities is contained in the eleventh to the twenty-second books, the first three of which concern themselves with the Fall, the rejection of cyclicism (Bk. XII), and the nature of evil and resurrection.

Book XIV is particularly significant in that it describes the City of God which lives according to the will of God, and the

City of the World, a city based on pride, sensuality, and general dissipation of spirit. Grace and pride stand opposed. The two cities are built by two contrasting loves.

Books XV to XVIII follow the historical development of the two cities with specific attempts to identify personages and events in terms of their relationship to one or the other of the two cities. Prefiguration and symbol are used widely here. The City of the World in Abraham's time is Assyria; David and Samuel prefigure Christ; Rome is the new Babylon.

Books XIX to XXII detail the end of the two cities or the fruits of the two conflicting philosophies of life. The world is pictured as incapable of providing genuine happiness and peace which will be found in the beatific vision.

At the end of history the mystery of the human situation will be made clear; virtue will be eternally rewarded and vice eternally punished.

AUGUSTINE'S IMMEDIATE INFLUENCE

Continuing Augustine's work in the patristic period was Paul Orosius, born in Braga, Portugal, between 380 and 390 A.D. A young priest, very much a man of his world, Orosius was shipwrecked around 413 off the coast of Africa and went on to Hippo to meet Augustine. Although the object of their concern was doctrinal problems raised by the Priscillianists and Origenists in the early Church, their relationship was particularly significant in that it produced, at Augustine's request, the Seven Books of History Against the Pagans, a kind of supplement to the City of God.[22] Augustine felt that some themes were inadequately treated in the City of God, particularly since he relied exclu-

[22] This is particularly true of the theme of Bk. III, in which Augustine maintains that imperial Rome suffered as many calamities in the old regime as she did under the aegis of Christianity. Cf. Orosius, The Seven Books of History Against the Pagans, trans. by Roy J. Deferrari (Washington, D.C.: The Catholic University of America Press, 1964).

sively on the history of Rome from its origin to the birth of Christ. It was Augustine's wish that his young disciple expand the work to include the histories of all people of the ancient world who are seen as providentially directed by an all-wise God. The work was hurriedly written, superficial in treatment, unabashedly apologetic in character, yet it endured as a history textbook well into the Middle Ages.

Alfred the Great (849–899) made an Anglo-Saxon translation of the work, and Otto of Freising (1110–1158) and his contemporaries were evidently familiar with it. Otto himself is rather important as the author of *The Two Cities, a Chronicle of Universal History to the Year 1146, A.D.*, one of the most distinguished of the more than one hundred chronicles of universal history written from the time of Eusebius (c. 260–340) to Otto's time.[23]

Orosius, like Augustine, views the temporal process in terms of salvation history, but he is much more optimistic and sympathetic to both empire, which he sees as preserving Roman values without Roman rule, and to the barbarians whom he sees as capable of assimilating Roman and Christian values.

Orosius nevertheless sees history in terms of original sin and divine chastisement—a progression through Babylonian, Macedonian, African, and Roman eras to a general state of existence superior to pagan times. But he is always the man of faith, the believer, who knows that he has here no lasting city, and that union with God is his destiny. As Löwith says:

> To a Christian believer like Augustine or Orosius secular history is not meaningful in itself but is a fragmentary reflection of its supra-historical substance, the story of salvation, which is determined by a sacred beginning, center, and end.[24]

---

[23] Otto exhibited much less optimism than Orosius about the state of the world, although as bishop of Freising he was committed to a belief in Providence. He lived in the tumultuous period of the Second Crusade. Edessa, a center of Christianity in Asia Minor, had been taken by the Seljuk Turks. The papacy and empire were in conflict and the European powers themselves were in turmoil.

[24] Karl Löwith, *op. cit.*, p. 181.

The latter Christian theologies of history are, as we shall see, Augustinian in inspiration and linear in character. Despite the revival of cyclicism in the morphological determinism of Spengler and the "eternal return" theory of Nietzsche, Augustine's linearism was the historical style that was to endure, "trivialized," as Nietzsche said, in secular versions, but destined to form the outlook of the inquirer for centuries to come.

Suggested Readings

Vernon Bourke, *Augustine's Quest of Wisdom*, Milwaukee: The Bruce Publishing Company, 1945. Ch. XIII: "God and Society," pp. 248–284..

T. F. B. (compiler), *A Monument to St. Augustine*, London: Sheed and Ward, 1945. Christopher Dawson, "St. Augustine and His Age," pp. 15–77.

Charles N. Cochrane, *Christianity and Classical Culture*, New York: Oxford University Press, 1959. Ch. XII: "Divine Necessity and Human History," pp. 456–516.

Martin D'Arcy, *The Meaning and Matter of History*, New York: Meridian, 1959. Ch. V: "Providence," pp. 133–157; Ch. VIII: "The Two Cities," pp. 204–217.

J. N. Figgis, *The Political Aspects of St. Augustine's City of God*. New York: Peter Smith, 1921. This entire book should be read as background material.

Karl Löwith, *Meaning in History*, Chicago: University of Chicago Press, 1949. Ch. IX, X, XI, pp. 160–190. These chapters discuss Augustine, Orosius, and the Biblical View of History.

R. A. F. MacKenzie, *Faith and History in the Old Testament*, New York: Macmillan, 1966. Ch. V: "The Problem of Myth and History," pp. 69–81.

R. L. P. Milburn, *Early Christian Interpretation of History*, New York: Hillary, 1954. Ch. II: "The Use of History in Early Apologetic: Clement of Rome to Irenaeus," pp. 21–37.

Roger L. Shinn, *Christianity and the Problem of History*, New York: Bethany Press, 1953. Ch. II: "Some Leading Christian Ideas—With Help from St. Augustine," pp. 29–62.

J. T. Shotwell, *Introduction to the History of History*, New York: Columbia University Press, 1923. Ch. VII: "The Old Testament as History," pp. 79–86.

Marthinus Versfeld, *A Guide to the City of God*, New York: Humanities Press, 1958.

CHAPTER FOUR

VICO AND THE NEW SCIENCE

Among the most neglected of the truly great thinkers whose ideas anticipated the modern world is the distinguished Italian, Giambattista Vico (1668–1744), heralded by Goethe as a patriarch of modern thought.[1]

Vico brought the skills of a historian, the faith of a devout Christian, and the vision of a prophet to the task of forming a complete historical methodology and science of human society. It was Vico's aim in his *New Science* to write a history of the *mondo civile* in which history becomes not an antiquarian interest in the past for its own sake, but a scientific analysis of the life of people in their actual existential situation, an element to be stressed by the historicists in later centuries.

The *New Science* was an attempt to give a broad sociological basis to supplement traditional methods of historical inquiry by one who was interested not only in documentary history but in all of man's cultural institutions. It might also be considered an attempt to synthesize history and philosophy, philosophy and

---

[1] Even Frank E. Manuel, one of the most perceptive and certainly one of the best stylists writing in the field of philosophy of history, dismisses Vico as a Janus-like figure exhibiting the faces of a Renaissance humanist and a romantic philosopher of history "whom Michelet re-created in the nineteenth century." *Shapes of Philosophical History* (Stanford, Calif.: Stanford University Press, 1965), p. 47.

philology, and to consider cultural history the study of the successive psychological state of mind in different epochs. Philology to Vico is not limited to linguistics, but covers all recorded human events.[2] Vico seeks meaning in the cultural coherence of religion, law, politics, the arts, customs, and in language.

Löwith sees Vico as anticipating specifically the basic ideas of Herder, Hegel, Dilthey, Spengler, and "the more particular discoveries of Roman history by Niebuhr and Mommsen, the theory of Homer by Wolf, the reconstruction of ancient life through etymology by Grimm, the historical understanding of laws by Savigny, of the ancient city of feudalism by Fustel de Coulanges, and of the class struggles by Marx and Sorel." [3]

VICO'S LIFE AND BACKGROUND

Vico was born in Naples in 1661, the son of an impoverished bookseller. After an almost fatal accident in a fall from a balustrade at the age of seven, the formerly happy child became a quiet, introspective, brooding convalescent given to long hours of study in the one room apartment over his father's bookstore.[4]

The schooling of the precocious youth was rather erratic as he found little to challenge him in formal educational circles. Pri-

[2] *The New Science of Giambattista Vico*, trans. by T. G. Bergin and M. H. Fisch (Ithaca, N.Y.: Cornell University Press, 1948), p. 139. References here are to paragraph numbers which are similar in both English and Italian editions. This translation is based on the third (1744) Italian edition. For bibliographical information on Vico's writings, see Benedetto Croce, *The Philosophy of Giambattista Vico* (New York: Russell, 1964), Appendix IV, pp. 302–310.

[3] Karl Löwith, *Meaning in History* (Chicago: University of Chicago Press, 1946), p. 115. The author quotes Marx as finding in Vico "many a gleam of genius," and particularly the foundations of comparative philology. *Ibid.*, p. 240. For a Marxian critique of Vico, see M. Lifshitz, "Giambattista Vico," *Philosophy and Phenomenological Research*, VIII (March, 1948), pp. 391–414.

[4] *The Autobiography of Giambattista Vico*, trans. by M. H. Fisch and T. G. Bergin (Ithaca, N.Y.: Cornell University Press, 1963), pp. 109–209. Cf. also, Paul C. Perrotta, "Giambattista Vico, Philosopher-Historian," in *The Catholic Philosophy of History* (New York: Kenedy, 1936), pp. 189–236; H. P. Adams, *The Life and Writings of Giambattista Vico* (London: George Allen and Unwin, 1935); and Benedetto Croce, *op. cit.*, pp. 247–267.

vately, however, he read and studied far into the night, especially in medieval philosophy, which eventually proved so unrewarding that he abandoned all study for a year and a half.

His interest was elicited once again by his chance encounter with the literati of Florence at their favorite meeting place, the Academy of St. Lawrence. He consequently resumed study, concentrating on Plato, Zeno, Aristotle, and Scotus; but learning that Suarez had both adequately and clearly systematized philosophy, he spent a full year studying Suarezian philosophy.

Turning to a study of law, he covered the five-year university program in a much briefer time, gaining admittance to the bar at the age of sixteen. Shortly after, he achieved fame in Naples by defending his father in a civil suit, receiving the plaudits of his legal adversary, a well-known Neapolitan attorney.

A brief divigation into poetry occasioned by his distaste for the clamor of the law courts was interrupted by crippling tuberculosis. He was able to leave the fetid air of Naples for some nine years to tutor the nephews of the Bishop of Ischia in the beautiful climate and pleasant quiet environment of the family castle near Salerno.

From an early interest in Aristotle, whom he had come to know from studying Suarez, Vico became progressively interested in Plato and in the possibility of constructing, according to the pattern of an ideal eternal law, the science of human society.[5]

It is interesting to note that Vico is unfettered by an allegiance to a system—especially to the Cartesian system which was so much in vogue. He describes this independence of mind rather quaintly in the third person:

. . . Vico blessed his good fortune in having no teacher whose words he had sworn by, for he felt most grateful for those words

---

[5] At this period he pictures himself as admiring Plato, the man of esoteric wisdom, and Tacitus, the man of common wisdom. To these he adds the name of Francis Bacon, "a man of incomparable wisdom both common and esoteric." *The Autobiography*, p. 139.

in which, guided by his good genius, he had followed the main course of his studies untroubled by sectarian prejudice, for in the city taste in letters changed every two or three years like styles in dress.[6]

In 1723 he had failed to obtain a Chair of Law and reluctantly turned to philosophy and history, producing in 1725 a work that he felt would give an empirical and scientific character to history, awesomely entitled *Principi d'una Scienza Nuova d'intorno alla natura delle Nazioni*, which was mercifully shortened to the *Scienza Nuova* or *New Science*.

After the publication of his *New Science* in 1725, he found to his chagrin that he had "launched it upon a desert." Vico was still centuries ahead of his time, relatively unappreciated, and still poor.

He made his living writing odes, eulogies and histories, an irritating profession for a man who wished to be recognized as a scholar of depth and substance. But little by little the fame he secretly envisioned came to him. The *New Science* began to be read more widely, and its author began the first of seven revisions, all written in longhand.

Shortly after the induction of Charles III as King of Naples in 1734 Vico, an Italian, was given by his Spanish sovereign the title of royal historiographer. The comfort of which he was deprived by the poverty of his early years came to him at last. But by 1737 he was an invalid, and his son, Gennaro, who eventually succeeded his father at the University of Naples, substituted for him when necessary. He died in 1744 reciting a psalm of David, having received the last rites from his friend, Dom Nicola Merula.

Despite a dislike of scholastic orthodoxy which remained with him throughout his life, Vico was quite sympathetic to systematic presentation, and he combines the full resourcefulness of a creative synthesist with the scientific care of the scholarly investigator.

[6] *Ibid.*, p. 133.

It was no accident that he called his work the *New Science*. His approach was to be precisely that—new in that it was to be a rational construction of the civil world on a scale never before attempted, and a science inasmuch as it was to be the result of scrupulous inquiry and substantiated assertion. The *New Science* was also intended by the author to be "a rational civil theology of divine providence," an analysis of the institutions, customs, property, laws, tradition, and a history of ideas.

His methodological approach is that man knows best what he creates, and as man has created civil society he has the capacity to know it. Man's historical knowledge begins therefore with the structure of society as it actually is. He distinguishes three grades of knowledge: a lower kind of thought (*pensiero*) involving uncertainty and reflection; a superior and confident awareness of truth (*coscienza*) but without knowledge of causes; and the mental possession of truth through its causes (*scienza*). He maintains that God alone knows all things, that man is aware of many things but generally knowledgeable about only a few.[7]

The master plan of Vico's work is that of a philosophy of human society directed in its multiple domestic, social, political, artistic, and religious life by a beneficent providence. It is providence which directs all in a wholly admirable and wise fashion.

The width of this approach reveals the profoundly anti-Cartesian character of Vico's work. Descartes seeks certainty in a geometrical model of the clear and distinct idea from which subsequent truths may be correctly deduced. Historical inquiry, involving as it does both creative questioning and evidence that is not always amenable to mathematic verification, cannot hope to meet the narrow Cartesian norms of a science. Moreover, since universal history is almost inevitably interpretative, it involves a romanticism with which Cartesian mathematical methodology cannot effectively deal. Vico did not deny the possibility of Descartes' methodology arriving at truth; he did reject the

[7] Croce has the best analysis of Vico's theory of knowledge in the first two chapters of his classic study, *The Philosophy of Giambattista Vico*, pp. 1–35. Cf. also pp. 279–301.

claim that mathematical method yielded more than partial insights into reality.

Vico is neither unduly credulous nor skeptical. His sympathy for Bacon and Galileo give him an attitude toward empirical science that is neither deprecatory nor servile, but appreciative of the legitimate contributions of the experimental disciplines. But the ultimate justification for man's knowledge of history is the fact that he has made it. History is a human *factum*.

> . . . The world of civil society has certainly been made by men, and its principles are therefore to be found within the modifications of our own human mind. Whoever reflects on this cannot but marvel that the philosophers should have bent all their energies to the study of that world of nature, which, since God made it, He alone knows; and that they should have neglected the study of the world of nations or civil world, which, since men made it, men could hope to know.[8]

There is a progressive evolution in his epistemology from his fortieth year when he wrote his *De antiquissima Italorum sapientia*. His interests in law, religion, politics, and philology made him reflect more on the nature of man and man's history. History he sees as a product of man.

> Is not the creator of history simply man, with his ideas, his passions, his will, and his actions? And is not the mind of man, the creator of history, identical with the mind that is at work in thinking it and knowing it?[9]

As a consequence of this conviction, Vico sees history not as an elaboration of the clear and distinct idea, but the inevitable relationship between the event and man, its creator. Admittedly there is a similarity between Descartes and Vico in their common desire to dissociate self from the bias of habitual assumption based on fancy, wishful thinking, or prejudice. Empirical knowledge is valid but limited; Aristotelian logic is not neces-

---

[8] *The New Science*, 331.
[9] Benedetto Croce, *op. cit.*, p. 23.

sarily invalid but incapable of yielding true knowledge of reality. Vico's thought is personalistic, and he seems to have an existentialist's disdain for what he feels to be the pretension of both Cartesian scientism and Scholastic rationalism.

Nevertheless he is most interested in justifying the scientific character of his work, in writing a history that is more than a diary of heroes, didactic moralizing, apologetics, or chronologies of events and dynasties.[10]

Vico feels that historical inquiry suffers from certain fallacies to which the historian may be prone: an academic egocentrism which makes him exaggerate the overall importance of the area in which he happens to be interested; a nationalism which tends to make him less objective in evaluating the fatherland's triumphs and failures; a presumption of similarity between the academic mind of the historian and less reflective and differently motivated historical activist—who in fact is rarely the academic theoretician; the failure to recognize the possibility of the independent growth of similar ideas and institutions in different cultures; and the illusion of thinking earlier ages better informed than the contemporary historian about periods closer to them in time.[11]

Particularly ingenious in Vico's methodology is his interpretation of mythology as revealing an authentic primitive vision of the domestic, social, political, and religious life of ancient societies. Mythic representation develops in more sophisticated ages into more appropriate legal and ethical formulations, but myth, containing as it does germinal truth, is much more than legend. Vico also anticipates the morphological theory of cultural growth that was to become so popular in the nineteenth century by suggesting that we understand the process of a given society by analyzing the growth process of all societies.

The *New Science* is a combination of historical, philosophical, religious, legal, and sociological thought. As a history it sketches

---

[10]Cf. *The Autobiography*, Ch. III, pp. 20–46.
[11] These fallacies were probably inspired by Bacon's "idols" to which they bear a certain resemblance. Cf. Croce, *op. cit.*, pp. 155–158.

such subjects as the cultural development of primitive people, the rise of civilization, Greco-Roman class struggles, democratic political theory, and medieval life. As a philosophy it contains an epistemology, an ethics, a phenomenology of religion and a rational psychology. As legal philosophy it demonstrates that "the natural law is the radical synthetic principle of the total juridical actuality." [12] As a sociology it contains detailed descriptions of social events, personalities, relationships, and their involvement with language, law, and institutional political forms.

The first version of 1725 was rewritten with considerable additions in 1730, and the first version itself is the culmination of earlier writings in metaphysics, anti-Cartesian epistemology, and reflections on legal and social structures.[13] Its subject is man, wounded by original sin, making his way under educative providential direction to his last end. God is provident, but man is the creator of the civil order, and his history is to be found in the history of man's mental states as they articulate themselves in cultural institutions.

CYCLE THEORY

Vico pictures his *New Science* as describing "at the same time an ideal eternal history traversed in time by the history of every nation in its rise, peoples, maturity, decline, and fall." [14] His was far too analytic and critical a mind to accept the carelessly

---

[12] A. Robert Caponigri, *Time and Idea: The Theory of History in the Thought of Giambattista Vico* (Chicago: Henry Regnery, 1953), p. 39.

[13] Cf. H. P. Adams, *op. cit.*, p. 147; and Croce, *op. cit.*, Ch. III, "Internal Structure of the *New Science*," pp. 36–43. The name of the *New Science* was inspired by Bacon's *Novum Organum* and Galileo's *Dialoghi delle Nuove Scienze*. F. Nicolini, who wrote *La Giovinezza di Giambattista Vico*, produced the famous 1744 edition which indicates the textual differences of all editions produced up until that time. The most complete bibliographical source on Vico is the *Bibliografia Vichiana*, Bari: 1911. The project was initiated by Benedetto Croce and continued by Fausto Nicolini. Supplements were published in 1927, 1932, 1936, and 1940. A revised supplement in two volumes was published by Nicolini in 1947–48 under the editorship of Riccardo Ricciardi.

[14] *The New Science*, 349.

assembled chronicles that often repeated the same faulty sources and perpetuated the same legends.

Vico's was political history in the sense that the nation is the collectivity that includes the vast range of ideas, activities, and institutions—and thus is a basic historical structure.

The development of the nation is charted through divine, heroic, and civil phases.[15] But individual development presupposes a broader division of all time into the eras of the obscure, the fabulous, and the historical.[16]

Obscure time is characterized by an earlier period in the history of humanity in which human culture begins in early nature religion and finds expression in primitive theologies. Judgment was sought from the gods in the absence of legal or juridical structures. Society is by its very nature transitional, and cultural residues inevitably exist in some form in later social forms.[17] Earlier primitive peoples build cities for the gods, later peoples for themselves. The heroic age is already taking shape before the end of the obscure period, and endures through the age of fable and state-building.

Obscure time develops from the theocratic period when family organization predominated to the time of the larger social forms of kingdoms and republics.

The fabulous period is the age of symbol and story when reality is understood in terms of fables to which Vico hopes to

[15] *Ibid.*, p. 916.
[16] Martin D'Arcy summarizes well the rather confusing divisions of Vico: "Using his knowledge of law and philology he gathered the evidence for his theory from language, literature, custom, law and religion, and depicted history as the long story of how man becomes human in the high sense of the word. He distinguishes three stages; in terms of literature, the periods of the god, the heroes and men; in terms of man's faculties, the periods of sense, imagination and reason; in terms of law, chaos and custom, external authority and rational obedience. The changes come about, partly through the free will of man, and partly through the force of choices and circumstances outside man's will. 'Humanity is man's own work, with tragic overtones of failure.' " *The Meaning and Matter of History* (New York: Meridian, 1959), p. 124.
[17] This contrasts sharply from the morphological cyclicism of Spengler which presupposes discontinuity of cultures and replaces causality by destiny. Vico considers causality as a regulative agent in historical change. Cf. also Croce, *op. cit.*, Ch. XIV: "History of Obscure Periods," pp. 154–164; Caponigri, *op. cit.*, p. 124.

provide the key by understanding the thought forms of the period. The historical period Vico records as beginning during the Second Punic War (218–201 B.C.) when Rome was engaged in the great task of humbling Carthage.

This primitive period of humanity is "divine" in the sense that it is culturally oriented around religion. The language is a mélange of pre-scientific myths and poetry older than Homer, suggestive of pantheism.[18]

The heroic period is the period of the warrior hero, the age of poetry and imagination and agricultural society, an age of force tempered by religion.

Both divine and heroic periods are activist and spontaneous as opposed to the civil which is reflective and classical in tone.

Vico's theory of *ricorso* or recurrence suggests that the process begins anew, a new structure rises phoenix-like from the ashes of the old.[19]

Thus the first age of the gods is the period of divine governance, an age which combines poetry and cruelty, fear and awe, and a generally primitive level of existence. It has its primitive kind of law and hieroglyphic mode of expression.

The second is the heroic age or the age of the powerful and prestigious warrior aristocracy and its corresponding legal and social apparatus. The hero is strident, often cruel, and roughly assertive. At first there is no law by which he is restrained, so the duel and vendetta become the arbiters of conflict. Contract in a moneyless society is by common agreement; language is colorful, imprecise, figurative, and symbolic. Vico suggests that in this period providence restrains the bestial tendencies of

---

[18] One notes the similarity of this division to the law of the three stages of Auguste Comte (1798–1857). Comte in 1822 formulated in a paper he later called his *opuscule fondamental* his thesis that human knowledge necessarily passes through three successive stages: the theological or fictitious stage; the metaphysical or abstract stage; and the positive or scientific stage. The theological stage is an age of ignorance in which reality is interpreted in terms of continuous and frequently capricious divine intervention. Cf. Henri de Lubac, *The Drama of Atheist Humanism* (New York: Sheed and Ward, 1949), pp. 79–84. It might be noted further that Comte admired Vico and mentions him in a letter to John Stuart Mill in 1844.

[19] Cf. *The New Science*. Book V treats of the *ricorso* and its nature.

powerful heroes who gradually take on the prestige originally accorded to the gods. Their power is thought to be divine in origin, and the plebeians accommodate their lesser life to this authority structure.[20]

The third period is the most distinctively human, representing a felicitous blend of conscience and duty, with particular reference to the civil order. Government develops from its aristocratic phase to recognize the freedom and equality of men. Language in this period develops in both complexity and precision, but incorporating the vivid imagery of the heroic period.

In this way, Vico outlines the cycle of three ages in each *corso*. History in general, and nations in particular have followed this order. The path begins in obscure times, passes through the age of fables in the ages of recorded history, and into the plenitude of human reason.[21]

With each period of historical development there are distinctive customs, laws, economies, literatures, and art which constitute a distinct culture.[22]

The *corso* finally ends with a descent into a new barbarism, a "barbarism of reflection" in which thought has spent itself and endures only in a sterile pedantry and craftiness. This new barbarism is worse than the primitive kind, involving as it does rationalization of malice, war, and strife.[23]

Not only does Vico, in his theory of historical residues, allow for a certain continuity of cultural elements, but he seems to allow for a creative dialectical tension which permits the processes of cultural adaptation and assimilation.

[20] Vico's work is inferior here to the classic study of ancient institutions by Numa de Fustel de Coulanges, * The Ancient City (New York: Doubleday, 1956).

[21] Lawrence J. Czechowicz, An Analysis of the Theory of Cycles of Giambattista Vico (Washington: Catholic University of America Press, 1961), p. 28. Cf. also Thomas M. Berry, The Historical Theory of Giambattista Vico (Washington: Catholic University of America Press, 1949).

[22] The New Science, Book IV, pp. 283–347.

[23] Compare this to the distinction made later by Nicholas Berdyaev (1874–1948) between primitive and civilized barbarism. Cf. Slavery and Freedom (New York: Charles Scribner's Sons, 1944).

It is important to recognize in Vico that the *corsi* are not independent cultural entities undifferentiated by accumulated experience. Vico recognized the acquired intellectual capital of past ages as giving color and substance to subsequent historical *corsi*. Recurring ages are not mere repetitions of each other, but are moving, as has been observed, in a providential direction. There is also an interesting interplay between the histories of individual nations and universal history itself.

The past lives in the present but is harmoniously absorbed and qualitatively improved by it. Individual nations have histories that represent distinct historical developments, but there is a broad contemporaneity and eventual unity by which they are related.

The term *ricorso* or recurrence has caused some confusion among commentators on Vico because of the difference of opinion that exists concerning the exactitude of the repetition of historical events. Cyclicism in Vico is quite obviously not the Stoic type that would see historical identities reappear with inflexible regularity. But the whole path from sensation and imagination to reason, and from force to justice is destined to recur again and again. The barbarism of reflection will yield in time to a new barbarism of sensation, and the process will begin anew.

Vico does not see the *ricorso* in terms of deterministic astronomical necessity but "according to the rhythm of the elementary forms of the mind." It is in this sense that history is the history of mental states rather than a diary of events. A people moves from their primitive condition to political organization. Psychologically they respond successively to need, utility, convenience, luxury, and end in dissipation of creative energies. It was not possible for Vico to work out a complete periodization that would admit of no exceptions, for his Christian linearism would preclude the possibility of nature reassembling itself in exact temporal configurations.

What is significant here is that Vico's theory of the *ricorso* is quite compatible with a theory of progress which is symbolized adequately by neither line nor circle, but by an ascending spiral, representative of a continuous cultural development and enrichment. Vico never formulated such progressivist theory in the manner of Condorcet or Turgot. Certainly in his preoccupation with multiple developments in history he never approaches a pantheistic identification of natural and supernatural elements; nor, despite certain resemblances to Hegel, is he guilty of a reductionism in which the supernatural God of Christian theology is by-passed in favor of an all-enveloping Absolute Spirit. For he despised pantheism, and was much too traditional theologically to anticipate later Hegelian religious thought. Yet it is certainly true that Vico, like Hegel, was aware of the relevance of social institutions as articulations of the spiritual.

It may well be that Vico's essential fame rests more on his ability to see and formulate the interrelated problems of his world than to give definitive answers to the problems raised. Croce accuses him of "fanciful etymologies, erroneous citations of names, dates, and quotations, and faulty mythological interpretations." [24] He denies that Vico had an acute mind in philosophy or that his historical work was truly critical, accusations which appear to be justified only by the application of the more exalted standards of late nineteenth-century historical scholarship.

It has been said too that Vico had the parochial prejudice of the superiority of the Latin mind, that he ignored Eastern culture (as most philosophers of history writing in the West tend to do), and that he made errors in philological derivation. But for a man who anticipated so much of what was to come, his faults seem minimal.

Vico is not formally recognized as a maker of the modern mind, but the student of the history of ideas is fascinated by the inter-disciplinary approach to the secular world in all of its richness by a man who seemed so removed from its turmoil in his own time. Vico as a cultural historian contributes a liberating methodology that extends the field of inquiry horizontally to

[24] Croce, op. cit., p. 152.

include anything authentically human, and vertically, to investigate origins and providential destiny.

One might indeed question the validity of answers given in such fields as philology, philosophy, and history, without rejecting the enormous synthetic construct by which the world's disciplines are seen both in their relatedness to each other and in terms of their relation to God.[25]

Croce sees Vico as the nineteenth century in germ and suggests some of his more significant contributions, while recognizing his almost non-existent contribution to a philosophy of progress.

> But if in this point Vico cannot stand comparison with later philosophy, the failure is amply atoned for by the full agreement between his historical discoveries and the criticism and research of the nineteenth century. Above all, he agrees with his successors in his rules of method, his scepticism as regards the narrative of ancient historians, his recognition of the superiority of documents and monuments over narrative, his investigation of language as a store-house of primitive beliefs and customs, his social interpretation of mythology, his emphasis on spontaneous development rather than external communication of civilisation, his care not to interpret primitive psychology in the light of modern psychology . . .[26]

He compares Vico with Leibniz, and sees the latter speaking to his own century which echoes his words far and wide, and the former as addressing his words to a wilderness. But he sees too the intrinsic character of thought undiminished by the fewness of the hearers. Vico, however, had his hearers, but they were not of his own time. The miracle was not in the fewness of the hearers in his own time, but in the capacity of those words to endure and live in the thought structure and institutions of future centuries.

[25] Vico rejected the notion of a people without God, calling it merely the gossip of travelers from obscure lands. For a detailed critique of Vico's thought, see Croce, *op. cit.*, Ch. XX, "Vico and the Later Development of Philosophical and Historical Thought," pp. 236–244.

[26] *Ibid.*, pp. 241–242. Cf. also *The Autobiography* . . . pp. 61–108; Adams, *op. cit.*, pp. 207–222.

Suggested Readings

I PROVIDENCE IN VICO

Benedetto Croce, *The Philosophy of Giambattista Vico*, New York: Russell, 1964, Ch. X: pp. 112–121.

M. C. D'Arcy, **The Meaning and Matter of History*, New York: Meridian, 1959, pp. 122–157.

The Autobiography of Giambattista Vico, trans. by M. H. Fisch and T. G. Bergin, Ithaca, N.Y.: Cornell University Press, 1963, pp. 46–60.

Karl Löwith, **Meaning in History*, Chicago: University of Chicago Press, 1946, pp. 115–136.

II VICO'S THEORY OF HISTORY

H. P. Adams, *The Life and Writings of Giambattista Vico*, London: George Allen & Unwin, 1935, Ch. XIII, pp. 147–171.

Thomas M. Barry, *The Historical Theory of Giambattista Vico*, Washington: Catholic University of America Press, 1949.

A. Robert Caponigri, *Time and Idea: The Theory of History in Giambattista Vico*, Chicago: Henry Regnery, 1953, Ch. III: "The Science of Humanity," pp. 55–70; Ch. VI: "Ideal Eternal History and the Course of the Nations in Time," pp. 109–129.

R. G. Collingwood, *The Idea of History*, London: Oxford University Press, 1946, pp. 63–71.

Benedetto Croce, *The Philosophy of Giambattista Vico*, New York: Russell, 1964, Ch. XIII: pp. 144–153.

III THE "RICORSI" IN VICO

A. Robert Caponigri, *Time and Idea: The Theory of History in Giambattista Vico*, Chicago: Henry Regnery, 1953, Ch. VI: "Ricorsi," pp. 130–143.

Benedetto Croce, *The Philosophy of Giambattista Vico*, New York: Russell, 1964, Ch. XI: "The Law of Reflux," pp. 122–133.

The New Science, trans, by M. H. Fisch and T. G. Bergin, Ithaca, New York: Cornell University Press, 1963. Book V, pp. 349–372.

CHAPTER FIVE

HISTORY AND THE PHILOSOPHY

OF PROGRESS

Man, as optimist, views human experience as a constant accumulation of wisdom and knowledge. He sees man as perfectible and his institutions as reflecting an ascending linearism that apotheosizes time rather than causality, and makes tomorrow inevitably superior to today.

The philosophy of progress was perhaps the greatest single factor in the development of the philosophy of history as a distinct, intellectual discipline in the eighteenth century, and one of the most significant trends in nineteenth century social theory.

Essentially, the philosophy of progress was a product of the Enlightenment, a rationalist effort for a planned revolution based upon the thinker's knowledge of the nature of human and social development. Voltaire's *La philosophie de l'histoire* of 1765 was significant, not because it was a great work in interpretative history, but because it ushered in a historical thought style, a synoptic view of perfectible man and his perfectible institutions. The strange survival of universal history based on inexact chronologies finally yielded precedence to the worldview in which the historical process itself and its direction became the object of critical scrutiny.

It might be thought rather arbitrary to choose certain key figures to concentrate on in the philosophy of progress, particularly since the notion of progress is always present in the empirical tradition.[1] To be sure, the works of Bacon, Locke, and Hume are good examples of philosophies based on the supposition that man learns from experience and moves constantly. But the philosophers of history are not interested in the isolated phenomenon of progress, but in progress as a cultural dynamic that structures the historical process itself. The philosophy of progress found expression in the thought of Herder, Lessing, Kant, and Hegel, but it was in a French tradition that it was to achieve its most significant form.

Vico, of course, had already initiated the process in the *New Science*, although oddly enough he did not develop a theory of progress beyond asserting that in the *ricorso* there is an accumulation of experience that is not mere repetition of what has gone before.

The argument as to whether Vico or Voltaire is the founder of the philosophy of history is not so important as the fact that their respective approaches in the eighteenth century inaugurated sweeping and creative attempts to extract meaning from the historical process as a whole. In Kant, Turgot, Condorcet, Saint-Simon, Comte, and Marx we have classic examples of the form progressivistic thought was to take. And the French Revolution was to provide the chief political context in which the *philosophes* were to formulate their vision of a society that was moving into a future of limitless possibilities, exorcised by the Renaissance and to some extent by the Reformation of its original religious elements, but retaining both its religious fervor and essential form. In Comte the religious accoutrements are bizarre, in Marx they are latent, in Condorcet they are absent— but in all varieties they retain the linear form of Augustine, Orosius, Otto of Freising, Joachim, and Bossuet.

[1] In a more detailed study of the philosophy of progress, Herder and Fichte would inevitably merit consideration.

KANT

Three years after Condorcet published his famous *Esquisse* (1794), in Prussia the aging Immanuel Kant (1724–1804) posed the question of progress in the *Disputation of the Faculties*, seeing man as either subject to progressive corruption, inevitable improvement, or imprisoned within the periphery of a circle of recurrent experience. The corruption theory was based upon the apprehensions of religious fundamentalists who saw the world decaying, and quasi-scientists who saw the machine of the world running down. Kant disliked both the negativism of the corruptionists and staticism inherent in cyclic recurrence, in favor of a eudaemonism which admitted the possibility of a qualified progress without suggesting its inevitability.[2]

In two earlier works, *The Idea of a Universal History from a Cosmopolitical Point of View* (1784) and *On the Common Saying* (1793), Kant developed his historical theory that mankind moves forward slowly even if no rational purpose can be readily discerned. The natural capacities of man he saw as gradually manifesting themselves in time. Nature provides a creative tension in the conflicts of men, which, when suitably resolved, become the causal principle of an ordered civil society; man's history is illustrative of the realization of a plan of nature itself to develop the ideal state in which the potential capacities of man may be most fully realized.

There is here an interesting similarity to Hegel, both in Kant's idea of the state as a political goal of nature, and in the creative antagonism of the dialectic created by man's natural "unsocial sociability." That is, man has simultaneously the urge to sociability and the urge for isolated independence, and from

---

[2] Cf. Josef Pieper, *The End of Time* (New York: Verry, 1954), pp. 88–105; S. Axinn, *A Study of Kant's Philosophy of History* (Philadelphia: 1955); and J. Bronowski and Bruce Mazlish, *The Western Intellectual Tradition* (New York: Harper and Row, 1962), Ch. XXVI, "Kant and Hegel: The Emergence of History," pp. 472–490.

the awareness of struggle within himself, he becomes progressively aware of the social antagonisms which lift him from his natural indolence to strive for honor, success, and wealth in the marketplace. Nature is so structured that these creative tensions take on organizational characteristics and, as man progressively realizes his capacities, the stable political society evolves.

Kant feels that progress is actually accelerated by a sharper conflict, somewhat in the fashion of a Toynbee two centuries later who posits a "stimulus of penalization" as part of a dialectic of growth.[3]

In Kant world progress is bound up with world peace. Warfare dissipates both human and financial resources. The state exists by means of a felicitous combination of coercive power and personal liberty, and nature's thrust toward a harmonious world community will represent mankind's most meaningful progress once morality has been more sedulously cultivated.

In short, Kant pictures the human race as advancing toward culture as its natural purpose, "continually making progress for the better"; and although this inexorable progress toward the better may be arrested, it will never be completely stopped.

EARLY FRENCH PHILOSOPHERS OF PROGRESS

It was in France, however, that the philosophy of progress had its most meaningful development, particularly in the seventeenth and eighteenth centuries. Even as early as 1525, Rabelais' Gargantua in a letter to Pantagruel expresses the mood in rejoicing at the expansion of knowledge, the availability of libraries, and the general rise in the level of learning. And in 1688, Bernard Bouvier de Fontenelle (1657–1757) in his *Digression on the Ancients and Moderns* expounded his theory of the indefinite

---

[3] Goethe too has suggested that unharassed human effort seeks too low a level. The idea is also emphasized in James and Whitehead. Cf. Howard Becker and Harry Elmer Barnes, *Social Thought from Lore to Science* (New York: Dover, 1961), p. 264.

expansion of knowledge and the perfectibility of human nature.[4]

A similar theme is to be found in *Observations on the Continuous Progress of Reason* by the Abbé de Saint Pierre published in 1737. The Abbé also saw the future in terms of limitless possibility for the expansion of knowledge, happiness, social reform, and world peace.[5] His *Project to Perfect the Government of States* (1773) is the chief source for his sketch of the progressive nature of civilization. He sees progress made more meaningful by the expansion of communications, maritime commerce, the rise of the empirical sciences, and the invention of printing.

Even earlier, in the latter half of the sixteenth century, Jean Bodin (1530-1596) suggests a world history divided into three periods characterized by religion, practical knowledge, and inventive genius respectively. History he represents as dependent on the free will of man active in a changing world which gives evidence of a rhythm of progress and retrogression, and in which man gradually improves his situation.[6] Bodin's principal preoccupation was the problem of human knowledge which he sees as subject to the cultural vagaries of rise and fall; he did not attempt to play the prophet, but felt that his contemporaries had expanded the frontiers of knowledge far beyond any expectation of the ancient world.

Turgot

The most significant names in the history of the theory of progress in France are Anne Robert Jacques Turgot (1727-

---

[4] Cf. J. B. Bury, *The Idea of Progress* (New York: Peter Smith, 1955), Ch. V, "The Progress of Knowledge: Fontenelle," pp. 98-126. This classic work on the subject of the nature, growth, and historical significance of the idea of progress is, despite its rather uncritical appraisal of Augustianism, a valuable source book for the historical personalities in the field. For a Christian appraisal of the problem, see Christopher Dawson, *Progress and Religion* (New York: Doubleday, 1960). Cf. also Etienne Gilson, *The Spirit of Medieval Philosophy* (New York: Sheed & Ward, 1940), Ch. XIX, "The Middle Ages and History," pp. 383-402.

[5] *Ibid.*, Ch. VI, p. 127.

[6] Cf. Robert Flint, *Philosophy of History* (New York: 1894), pp. 190-199.

1781), the Marquis de Condorcet (1743–1794), and Auguste Comte (1798–1857).

Turgot is in a sense the pioneer in progressivist theory, and with him the idea of progress, as Caro says, became for the first time "the organic principle of history." His friend and protegé, Condorcet, is heavily dependent on his teacher, and he anticipated (as did Vico a little earlier) in his *Discourse on the Successive Progress of the Human Mind* Comte's law of the three stages of the progress of mankind.[7] Turgot abandoned an early interest in theology for a political career, but he never lost his interest in theoretical problems of economics and history. Turgot associates worship of the gods with a period in which the connection of physical facts are not known by primitive man. He sees philosophers as recognizing the fanciful character of theological fables and replacing them with equally unsatisfactory abstract metaphysical theorizing. It is only in the later period when nature yields her secrets to scientific inquiry that man truly understands.

Turgot differentiates nature and history, seeing the empirical sciences as concerning themselves with the more or less regular and recurrent happenings in nature, and history concerning itself with the progressive and enlarging capital of accumulated experience. Turgot, who was scientifically knowledgeable, tried to find in the study of society an objectivity comparable to empirical verification. Like Vico, he recognized the role of language in the development of civilization, had a relatively sophisticated view of the relationship of human development to physical agencies, acknowledged the occasionally recessive character of human endeavor, and saw mistakes and evil as parts of a dialectic of experience by which man slowly learns. While recognizing the inequalities existent among men in an age about to produce revolution, he encouraged the development of the free society and the curtailment of aristocratic privilege.

[7] Turgot had the idea for the *Discourse* as a youth of twenty-three. He developed his ideas in two lectures delivered at the Sorbonne in 1750. Condorcet's *Esquisse d'un tableau historique des progrès de l'esprit humain* of 1794 is similar in content.

CONDORCET

The Marquis de Condorcet (1743–1794) reminds one of the guilt-ridden wealthy intellectual who embraces Marxism. An aristocrat, he welcomed the aristocracy's downfall in the French Revolution as the beginning of a great new era, even though as an aristocrat hiding in a garret he could see his friends being guillotined. Like Turgot he was interested in giving an empirical foundation to the social sciences, and from history he hoped to derive the basic social facts that would be the foundation of an objective science of society. He affirms a belief in progress, but is concerned too with an analysis of its nature, the direction it takes, and the form he believes it to assume in future years. He is interested in describing the ten successive phases of human society, the influence of one phase of development upon the other as man advances into the future sunlight of truth and happiness.[8] His fundamental conviction is that man has advanced uninterruptedly since making his appearance on earth. Human perfectibility manifests itself in continuous progress.

In short, Condorcet considered his *Esquisse* a map by means of which mankind would see where it had been, where it was, and where it was going. He traces man's progressive history in three primitive periods, starting with the tool-using primitive hunter and fisherman (nurturing the illusions of gods and personal immortality), the organization of classes in society based on the progressive control of property and food supply (the pastoral state), and the further stratification of society based upon wealth and power (the agricultural state). Progress even in this primitive phase is not a matter of the advancement of states, but the advancement in knowledge; and it is this advancement of knowledge that Condorcet considers the key to the progress of the human race. In the next period Condorcet recognizes Greek

---

[8] The intellectuals of the eighteenth century were often cautious in espousing progress. Lord Chesterfield, that indefatigable peddler of advice, could warn his son in 1748 to "speak of moderns without contempt and ancients without idolatry; judge them all by their merits but not by their ages."

culture and the contribution it made to the philosophy, art, and science of the western world. The next is the age of the Romans and the period of the empire's establishment of political institutions. Like Gibbon he laments the rise of Christianity as a repressive, anti-cultural force. Consequently his treatment of the medieval period is unsympathetic to its principal dynamic, religion. Scholasticism he considered an arid intellectualism. More significant than the development of commerce or the invention of gunpowder was the invention of printing, which guaranteed the diffusion of knowledge in an unprecedented manner. He sees particular significance in Newton's science, Locke's theory of human nature, and Rousseau's theory of society. His last stage was the era introduced by the French Revolution of his own time—an era that would see the realization of political and social equality, harmony among the world's powers, a great dissemination of knowledge, and the greatest happiness the human family had ever known.[9]

Of particular interest is the tendency of Condorcet to equate progress with scientific and technological sophistication, a progress formula that was to be later employed by Condorcet's spiritual son, Auguste Comte. The science that was especially important, as James Harvey Robinson has observed, was biology, which inadvertently instructed the historians in the genetic or developmental attitude which has figured so prominently in the "new" history.[10]

The importance of Condorcet is not to be found in the genius of his division of history, for his ten stages are somewhat

[9] William Godwin, in 1793, published a similar philosophy in his *Political Justice*, a work which espoused a progressivism based on the strength of political and social institutions. Crane Brinton cites the amusing example of Godwin's anarchy in the writer's dislike of an orchestra conductor's beating the time as an unwarranted tyranny over the orchestra members!

[10] Cf. Harry Elmer Barnes, A *History of Historical Writing* (New York: Dover, 1962), Ch. XV, "The New History and the Future of Historical Writing," pp. 373-404. The new history is an attempt to question the adequacy of history as past politics "anecdotally selected and episodically expounded," in favor of a mode of historical exposition which attempts to analyze and reconstruct the total history of the human experience. It presupposes, of course, considerable knowledge of anthropology and sociology.

arbitrarily selected, but in his awareness of the genetic method of describing human experience long before a Darwinian era when it was fashionable to do so, and long before anthropological, psychological, and sociological discoveries could indicate just how rich the developmental approach actually could be.

Although his master Turgot was sympathetic to the civilizing influence of Christianity, Condorcet was, in the tradition of Voltaire and Diderot, interested in shaking the altars with one hand and the thrones with the other.[11]

SAINT-SIMON

Count Henri de Saint-Simon (1760–1825) also figures prominently in progressivistic thought. A youthful exponent of revolutionary reform, he fought in the American Revolution, was imprisoned for almost a year during the Reign of Terror, and returned (having renounced his title) to devote his life to problems of social and political reform. His work was significantly extended by a young scholar who served for seven years as his personal secretary and who was destined to achieve greater fame than his mentor, Auguste Comte.

Saint-Simon picturesquely describes the golden age of the future as the perfection of the social order. "Our fathers have not seen it; our children will arrive there one day, and it is for us to clear the way for them."

It was his view too that the social, economic, and political upheaval of his age demanded a true science of cultural progress, a true *science politique*. Though liberally oriented, he was chagrined by the negativism and destructiveness of the French Revolution; it was his hope to become the Newton of the social sciences, and to reduce the problems of men in society to ascertainable laws.

[11] Bury, nevertheless, while acknowledging Turgot's acceptance of Providence, confesses that God resembles an honorary president who might be retired without affecting the proceedings of civilization. Bury, *op. cit.*, p. 207.

Progressively, he became less a theoretician and more a technologist and political analyst. Saint-Simon agreed with Condorcet that history enables us to see the future, and that history is charted by the progress of knowledge, although the former disagreed with his master in asserting that religion could not be ignored as a meaningful social phenomenon in the history of progress.

He combines his progressivism with a cyclic "law" of alternating organizational and revolutionary periods. The thrust, however, is in the direction of social happiness, not achieved by libertarian rhetoric but by scientific socialistic reorganization which he spelled out in great detail. In the organizational epoch men perceive a goal and fight to obtain it; in the revolutionary period they can see no goal and their efforts are ill-timed and uncoordinated.

It was Saint-Simon's idea to combine the social and empirical sciences in a synthetic science called "positive philosophy." [12] Such a science would capture the spirit of the age.

Comte

The most important seeker after a law of social progress was Auguste Comte (1798–1857), popularly regarded as the founder of sociology and a significant thinker in the analysis of progress and the historical process. To Saint-Simon he is indebted for many of his basic conceptions, particularly for his idea of the positive philosophy and the theory of correspondence of social and intellectual phenomena of a given age.[13]

Comte's philosophy was in a sense the crystallization of many independent currents of thought that would make of society a collective entity with its own ascertainable characteristics. The collapse of hope that accompanied the excesses of the French

[12] Saint-Simon uses this term popularized by Comte in his *Introduction to the Scientific Work of the Nineteenth Century.*
[13] Cf. Bury, *op. cit.*, p. 291.

Revolution, *le vandalisme révolutionnaire* as Despois called it, prompted in the nineteenth century the search for a more sober analysis of society that would supplement the partial insights of ideology, politics, economics.

Comte's new science of sociology was to permit the formulation of laws of growth that could be empirically verified.

A young mathematical scholar of considerable talent, Comte became the secretary of Saint-Simon after finishing the École Polytechnique in Paris. His early efforts to treat politics as a natural science presaged his future efforts to reduce society and its problems to a science with laws just as determinable as those of the physical sciences.

As indicated previously, the failure of the French Revolution to solve society's ills prompted the young intellectuals of the new century in France to seek a more stable order. The unprecedented diffusion of scientific knowledge prompted the young mathematician to explore the possibility of studying the phenomenon called society, not by conclusions drawn from theology or metaphysics, but from facts observed and analyzed, particularly those having to do with social change.

The early sociology was quite broad in scope, including the disciplines of politics, economics, anthropology, and social philosophy, although it was to develop into a specialized discipline that would confine itself to the study of the nature and function of social entities and the change to which they are subject.

Comte's *chef d'oeuvre* is his *Cours de philosophie positive* published from 1830–1842. In the early pages, he states his intention:

. . . The first characteristic of positive philosophy is that it views all phenomena as subjected to invariable natural laws. The purpose of our attempts—inasmuch as our search for causes, first or final, is vain—is to make an accurate discovery of those laws, and to reduce them to the smallest possible number.[14]

[14] The Harriet Martineau translation was published in 1855 under the title *The Positive Philosophy of Auguste Comte.*

The religious aspects of the new philosophy of positivism, perhaps motivated by Saint-Simon's *New Christianity*, are stressed in his *General View of Positivism*.

By far the most famous of Comte's ideas is his famous Law of the Three Stages in which he proposed that the human mind reaches maturity by passing through the stages of theology, metaphysics, and positive science. To Comte a man is a theologian in his childhood, a metaphysician in his youth, and a scientist in his manhood. The three stages represent not only the stages in the development of human thought, but the stages of development of the individual sciences as knowledge becomes progressively concrete.

In the first, the theological or "fictitious stage," primitive man ascribes all realities of the world to supernatural agents. Not only is this stage not to be condemned, it is to be recognized as an indispensable step in man's road to knowledge. But as an age of faith, it is a sign of primitive man's limitations.

In the second or metaphysical stage reason replaces blind faith and man begins to think in terms of causes, essences, and abstract principles. He sees phenomena previously ascribed to the gods as amenable to natural explanation, although philosophical exposition by reason of its own intrinsic limitation does not get down to the actual nature of things.

The period of maturity is the age of positive science when the mind seeks to discover the empirically verifiable laws that govern phenomena. This is the ultimate way of knowledge when the tangible and quantitative replace the vague and the abstract in human knowledge.

Comte specifies what he means by the scientific by a detailed analysis of subject matter. Of the four basic inorganic sciences of mathematics, astronomy, chemistry, and physics, mathematics is represented as the most basic and the one to which positive philosophy owes its origin and method.

The organic sciences are biology and social physics or sociology, whose objectivity is based on a methodology of observation, experimentation, and comparison. Social physics is the one science in particular that is needed to complete the system of the "sciences of observation." [15]

It is specifically from the technique of historical comparison of different coexisting social groups that progressivist thought emerges; for it is essential to Comte's system that societies be judged in terms of their historical development. His methodology, with its emphasis on the correct observation of phenomena, was not only a corrective to the more abstract theories of society, but also to a great degree set the thought style of the late nineteenth century.

The practical dimension of Comte's thought is emphasized in his contention that the function of sociology is to serve humanity in the social realities of its institutions and habits. All cultural entities have a vital and necessary relationship, so the study of social dynamics becomes a study of the progress of the whole of human society.

He develops his rather bizarre religion of humanity in *System of Positive Polity*, complete with a secular trinity of Humanity, Earth, and Space, a calendar of saints, and a unique liturgy. Order and progress, the theme of the new religion, is sought in political institutions; the seeker after scientific laws becomes the preacher of social salvation.

Comte was both a product and a maker of his times, for progress was perhaps one of the most durable of the convictions of the nineteenth-century Western mind, and the century before the outbreak of the first world war brought forth ample evidence to support the illusion. Science continued its brilliant march forward. It was particularly significant that the advances made in material culture—the conquering of distance, hunger, improvement of productive techniques, and the consequent mass output that would make these products more available to the average man—all of these factors made progress a reality to more than a social, political, and financial élite. Progress developed

[15] *Ibid.*, I, p. 12.

from a theoretical possibility into a mood, and from a mood into an assumption. As a mood it was sustained on the popular level by so many hundreds of improvements that it was suggested in 1876 that the Patent Office in the United States should be closed, as nothing more remained to be invented.

In addition to his influence on such individual figures as Mill, Durkheim, and Spencer, Comte made a profound impact on a generation, and he articulated well the positivistic preoccupation with the scientific, the material, the dimensive.[16] Emile Littré was to summarize this mood well when he said, "Whatever is beyond positive science is inaccessible to the human mind." Positive knowledge was the verifiable; all else was banished into the realm of inaccessibility.

It is a rather peculiar inversion of Comte's world that a scientifically sophisticated age has gone back to asking the ethical questions on which its survival may depend. Science cures and destroys with awesome brilliance, but unfortunately science cannot tell man which of the two he ought to do. And atomized knowledge has not yet succeeded in assembling itself into a meaningful context.

Positive philosophy was indeed to exercise an enormous influence over nineteenth-century thought, and Comte's was the most ambitious intellectual structure that the philosophy of progress was to take.

MARX

Karl Marx (1818–1883) is not ordinarily numbered among the classical figures in the philosophy of progress, but his economic determinism is equivalent to a kind of linear and secular

[16] John Stuart Mill was particularly impressed with the implications of Comte's thought for the cause of social and political liberalism, a central belief of which was "the conviction that human relations are amenable to intelligent understanding and control." Cf. George Sabine, A History of Political Theory (New York: Holt, 1950), p. 717.

salvation history.[17] Marx recognizes the significance of all of the cultural factors in history, but reserves the most active role to economics. In his concept of economic history he claims to have laid bare the dialectic of the historical process. History does not find its ultimate significance in an unfolding of an Hegelian Absolute Idea or Christian providence, nor in the deeds of philosophers or kings, nor in meaningless and spasmodic developments, but in a regular developmental dialectic determined by production. As he says in the Introduction to his *Critique of Political Economy*, "the mode of production in material life determines the general character of the social, political, and spiritual processes of life."

Marx was not interested in deriving models for historical understanding from plant morphology or from speculative systems. It has been said that he derived a dialectical methodology from Hegel, his sociology vicariously from Proudhon and Engels, and his materialism from Feuerbach. This is an oversimplification, but Marx does argue from a relativistic philosophy of becoming which is for him ontologically ultimate. His thought is derived from varied sources, and his materialism is basic to his system. Berlin considers Feuerbach "one of those authors, not infrequently met in the history of thought, who, mediocrities themselves, nevertheless happen to provide men of genius with the sudden spark . . ." [18] Marx himself identifies his philosophy as historical materialism in which class struggle is the social antithesis causing the rhythm of change to turn in the direction of the classless society.

It is not the individual—he is identified in the introduction of *Das Kapital* as a mere economic category—but the class which is

[17] For a good general study of Marx see Franz Mehring, *Karl Marx (Ann Arbor: University of Michigan Press, 1962), also, Isaiah Berlin, *Karl Marx, His Life and Environment (New York: Oxford University Press, 1959). An excellent critical bibliography is found in Berlin's book, pp. 269–273. Mandel Bober's Karl Marx's Interpretation of History, Vol. XXXI of the Harvard Economic Studies, originally published at Cambridge in 1948, is now available as a Norton paperback (1965).

[18] Berlin, *op. cit.*, p. 75. Marx's doctoral thesis in 1841 was an analysis of classical materialism as found in Epicurus and Democritus.

historically significant; and even the class does not "make" history, properly speaking. The freedom of the class is not the freedom to create the future but to recognize historical inevitability. This is the old concept of the *amor fati*, a recognition of inevitability that can facilitate or accelerate the process, but cannot change it.

The messianic and hortatory character of Marx's vigorous prose seems to pose a contradiction, since it might be presumed to be unnecessary to exhort men to act if the future were to be already determined. *Fata ducunt volentem, nolentem trahunt* reveals to man a kind of freedom which says little more than that he had better come quietly. Man does have a limited control of the material conditions of life, and it is from these material conditions of life that the entire culture of any society—law, politics, art, morals, and religion—ultimately depend. "It is not human consciousness that determines life; it is social life that determines consciousness."

The thesis of capitalism, a system created by the exploitative weapon of property and the accumulation of surplus value, finds its antithesis in an eventual rebellion against it, which in turn leads to the ultimate synthesis of the classless society—a state which Marx never satisfactorily describes.

Marx strangely enough despised utopias even as he posited the utopian dream of the classless society. He saw an inevitable process in which the abolition of private property would deprive man of the capacity to exploit; he saw after a time of temporary inequality the withering away of the state itself. In short, Marx, like Comte and Saint-Simon, is concerned with a science and not a theory of society, a science as exact as biology of which he, who fancied himself the Darwin of social science, would be the herald.

In nature . . . there are only blind unconscious agencies acting upon one another and out of whose interplay the general law comes into operation. . . . In the history of society, on the other hand, the actors are all endowed with consciousness. . . . But this distinction, important as it is for historical investigation, particularly of single epochs and events, cannot alter the fact that the course of history is governed by inexorable general laws . . . and it is only a matter of discovering these laws.[19]

In the tradition of Adam Smith and David Ricardo, Marx sees labor as the source of value; hence the emergence of the worker from his destitution will be dependent on his success in wresting control from the capitalists who amass the surplus value from the laborer's efforts.

Marx felt that even conscientious capitalists were forced by competition to rob the workers of the fruit of their labors, and he despised humanitarians and reformers for their efforts to preserve a system that he considered unworthy of preservation. He was sympathetic to political liberalism only to the extent that a bourgeois revolution—such as the French Revolution—is an indispensable step to the classless society.

It might also be noted that while Marxism in France and Germany was primarily a proletarian movement, in Russia it was a movement of "middle class intellectuals, for whom it became a kind of romanticism, a belated form of democratic idealism." [20]

Marx admitted not only the possibility of temporary inequality but a period of revolutionary strife. Although preferring political action, he would not agree with Michael Bakunin's advocacy of anarchistic violence. His tactic as contained in the *Communist Manifesto* of 1848 was to counsel a temporary alliance of proletariat with bourgeois democrats against the capitalistic establishment with the consequent hope of eliminating the temporary ally later.

Marx ordinarily was too obstreperous and explosive a personality to be diplomatic or devious, and concealment was not ordinarily a technique to which he was sympathetic. It was Lenin who was later to counsel, "It is necessary to go the whole length of any sacrifice . . . to resort to strategy and adroitness,

[19] Engels, *Selected Works*, 1942, p. 457.
[20] Berlin, *op. cit.*, p. 254.

illegal proceedings, subterfuge—to anything in order to pene-
trate." [21]

The relationship of Hegel to Marx has been the subject of
endless conjecture; while Marx retains the belief in a contra-
puntal interplay of forces, his well-known claim to have stood
the dialectic of Hegel on its head reveals his differences with the
latter's ideas on history's substance and direction. Hegel's idealistic myths yield to the harsh realities of the industrial world.

Karl Löwith has observed that Marx is first of all a philosopher
"with an immense historical sense" and a philosopher of history
less in his historical studies than in the *Communist Manifesto*
and *Das Kapital* in which class struggle, economics, and revolution are all absorbed into a comprehensive and unified historical vision.[22]

Marx's progressivism is not one of naive optimism, nor is it
the objectively scientific appraisal he would have it be. He feels
the God of history had been given the *coup de grâce* by such
stalwarts as Ludwig Feuerbach, for whom God was a mere projection of the finite. If, in the idiom of Luther, which was
developed by Hegel, popularized by Nietzsche (and carried into
the sixties by such modern theologians as Bonhoeffer, Altizer,
Hamilton, and Van Buren), God is dead, then the real task as
Marx saw it was to be concerned with the world at hand.

Marx's thought was a philosophy of history somewhat similar
in style to Hegel's but attributing significance to the proletarian
class that Hegel attributed to the state. The growth principle in
both systems is the clash of antagonistic forces of states (Hegel)
or of classes (Marx). There are stages of development in both,
and movement toward a goal. Though a materialist, Marx was
not satisfied with the mechanism used as a philosophic base for
the empirical sciences, nor did he have much sympathy for the
attempt by the natural scientist to introduce physical laws into
the fields of history and economics. His concept was indeed
evolutionary. The "non-coercive adjustments" democratically

---

[21] *Ibid.*
[22] Cf. Karl Löwith, *op. cit.*, p. 33.

arrived at in liberal political theory yield to progressive development generated by successive class conflicts.

As Professor Mayo, who has criticized Marxism specifically as
a philosophy of history, has observed, Marx had not the slightest doubt that he had made the process of history conscious, and
laid bare the laws of history themselves, although he was later
to protest against the "historico-philosophical theory of the
marche générale imposed by fate upon every people." [23] Mayo
quite legitimately questions Marxism as one would question any
single explanation for the reality that is history; he considers
Marx as underestimating non-economic factors and concentrating too exclusively on nineteenth-century conditions. If Engels
could object to the identification of bourgeois generalizations of
class viewpoint with eternal laws of nature, one can indeed object
to proletarian generalizations for the same reason. Mayo also
questions Marx's assumption that history moves forward in spiral
fashion by dialectical leaps, both on the grounds of the arbitrari-
ness of what progress may be thought to be and on the grounds
that the supposed progress is capable of satisfactory verification.[24]

Perhaps the most telling objection is the criticism that Marx
identifies the laws of nature and trends in society. He asserts
that the forces at work in society are exactly like the forces at
work in nature, and that they work violently, blindly, and de-
structively "as long as we do not understand them and fail to
take them into account." [25]

A final look at the philosophy of progress suggests that it was
the most significant development of nineteenth-century rationalism, a movement that grew with the growth of empirical

[23] Henry B. Mayo, *Introduction to Marxist Theory* (New York: Oxford University Press, 1960), p. 181. Cf. *Selected Correspondence of Marx and Engels,*
1846–1865 (London: 1934), p. 354.

[24] Mayo, *op. cit.,* pp. 188–189.

[25] Karl Popper sees Marx as a secular prophet inspired by a moral futurism,
preaching a gospel of dialectical necessity, and looking forward to a classless society as the beatific vision. Marx's is perhaps the most enduring and rationalistic
survival of the enlightenment philosophy of progress, combining with its rationalist elements an aura of myth. Cf. Karl Popper, *The Open Society and Its
Enemies* (New York: Harper Torchbooks, 1967), Vol. II, pp. 199–211.

science, political liberty, and a secularization that would emphasize the man of reason historically situated in the world.

Much of the cultural impetus of the movement was destined
to endure, particularly since empirical knowledge is by its nature
cumulative and progressive. But the new century with its wars,
totalitarian oppression, social injustice, and lawlessness was a
sober reminder that progress, either personal or collective, was
by no means inevitable or necessary.

Nicholas Berdyaev could castigate the theory of progress as
an exaltation of the future at the expense of the past and present
in the way that has not the slightest philosophic, scientific, or
moral justification; but it is more realistic to acknowledge with
Bury that for the intellectual community in the seventies and
eighties of the last century the concept of progress was an article
of faith in which the future was thought in some vague way to
be better than the past. Admittedly, the theory of progress in its
nineteenth-century form bore little resemblance to spiritual
progress as conceived by St. Augustine. But by the end of the
eighteenth century, scientific progress too had to share the stage
with the great libertarian social and political movements that
were taking shape. Progressivism was an inverted form of ancestor worship in which man worshipped his grandson rather than
his grandfather.

Perhaps the "law" which Kant, Condorcet, Saint-Simon, and
Comte sought was as elusive as the crock of gold at the rainbow's end, but man's increasing preoccupation—even in the religious community—with his world and its immediate problems
is a product of progressivism that is more meaningful today than
it has ever been.

To be disenchanted with a theory of inevitable progress, and
to despair ultimately in finding a law by which that progress may
be charted is not to say that human society cannot move forward.
It is merely to temper man's incorrigible optimism with the
sober reminder that what is possible is not necessary.

Suggested Readings

John Baillie, *The Belief in Progress*, Oxford: Saunders, 1950.

Harry Elmer Barnes, *A History of Historical Writing*, New York: Dover, 1962, pp. 174–176; *An Intellectual and Cultural History of the Western World*, Vol. II, New York: Dover, 1965, Ch. XX: "The Kingdom of Man and the Vision of Progress," pp. 823–843.

Carl Becker, *Progress and Power*, New York: Knopf, 1949.

Nicholas Berdyaev, *The Meaning of History*, New York: Peter Smith, 1946, Ch. X: "The Theory of Progress and the End of History," pp. 168–187.

Isaiah Berlin, *Karl Marx, His Life and Environment*, New York: Oxford University Press, 1959.

Mandel Bober, *Karl Marx's Interpretation of History*, New York: Norton, 1965.

J. B. Bury, *The Idea of Progress*, New York: Peter Smith, 1955, pp. 202–216 (Condorcet); pp. 238–253 (Kant); pp. 278–289 (Saint-Simon); pp. 290–307 (Comte).

Christopher Dawson, *Enquiries Into Religion and Culture*, London: Sheed, 1933, pp. 67–94; *Progress and Religion*, New York: Doubleday, 1960.

Ludwig Edelstein, *The Idea of Progress in Classical Antiquity*, Baltimore: Johns Hopkins University Press, 1969.

Sidney B. Fay, "The Idea of Progress," *American Historical Review*, 52, 1947, pp. 231–246.

Robert Flint, *Philosophy of History*, New York: 1894, pp. 88–104 (progress); pp. 280–289 (Turgot); pp. 325–339 (Condorcet); 395–408; 579–615 (Comte).

Morris Ginsberg, *The Idea of Progress*, Boston: Beacon Press, 1953.

Sidney Hook, *Marx and the Marxists*, New York: Van Nostrand, 1955. A valuable contrast of theoretical Marxism and its variant historical manifestations.

R. N. Carew Hunt, *The Theory and Practice of Communism*, London: Macmillan, 1963, Ch. IV: "The Philosophic Theory of Marxism," pp. 39–80.

Horace Kallen, *Patterns of Progress*, New York: Columbia University Press, 1950.

E. Kilzer, and E. J. Ross, *Western Social Thought*, Milwaukee: The Bruce Publishing Company, 1954, Ch. XIII: "Theories of Change and Progress," pp. 212–235.

Frank E. Manuel, *Shapes of Philosophical History*, Stanford, California: Stanford University Press, 1965, Ch. V: "The French Idea of Perfectibility," pp. 92–114.

Henry B. Mayo, *Introduction to Marxist Theory*, New York: Oxford University Press, 1960.

Franz Mehring, *Karl Marx, Ann Arbor: University of Michigan Press, 1962.

R. V. Sampson, Progress in the Age of Reason, Cambridge: Harvard University Press, 1956.

Preserved Smith, A History of Modern Culture, the Enlightenment, Vol. II, New York: Collier, 1966, pp. 202–211.

F. J. Teggart (ed.), The Idea of Progress, Berkeley: University of California Press, 1925; *Theory and Processes of History, Berkeley: University of California Press, 1962, Ch. VIII: "The Idea of Progress and the Foundations of the Comparative Method," pp. 82–98.

CHAPTER SIX

THE NEW CYCLICISM

When Thucydides in the fifth century B.C. maintained that accurate knowledge of the past was useful because "according to human probability, similar things will happen again," he was, as has been seen, expressing a typical viewpoint of the ancient world. Although there was no unanimous agreement on the precise inevitability of cyclic return, the Greco-Roman world did see experience in terms of eternally recurrent patterns, and it was a viewpoint that did not wholly die with the ancient world.

Löwith sees it as reappearing sporadically in the Middle Ages in the Aristotelianism of Siger of Brabant and in Dante's image of the Trinity as three revolving circles into which man is eventually absorbed (*Paradiso* XXXIII, 137 ff.); he also sees it in Part VIII of Hume's *Dialogues Concerning Natural Religion*, Fichte's *The Vocation of Man* (Part III, Ch. 4), and in Schelling's *The Ages of the World*.[1]

Although the doctrine of eternal recurrence is usually associated with a primitive thought-style based on an unsophisticated extrapolation from the world of nature to general cultural experience, it has survived in several influential modified forms in the modern world.

[1] Karl Löwith, *Meaning in History* (Chicago: Chicago University Press, 1949), p. 257.

This old thought-style was admirably adapted to the realities of the ancient world, which saw a wondrous regularity and rhythm in the forces of nature. To the Jews and Christians, history indeed became a kind of prophetism linearly directed to an eschatological goal, but the old patterns did not become extinct.

In such figures as Nietzsche, Danilevsky, Spengler, and Sorokin, we see examples of how cyclic theory has influenced differing historical outlooks and combined cyclic and progressivist elements to the point where fundamental identity becomes a question of basic emphasis. In Hegel, as we shall see, the combination of these elements reaches a point of ambiguity.

NIETZSCHE

In Friedrich Nietzsche (1844–1900) we have cyclicism revived on a purely materialistic basis. As reality is equivalent to its natural finite components, it is inevitable that, given an infinite duration, similar configurations of these basic building blocks would be inescapable—though not necessarily in inevitable sequence.[2] In adopting this classical thought-style, Nietzsche— despite his sympathy for Greek culture gained as a trained classical philologist under Friedrich Ritschl—never felt the security

[2] *The Complete Works of Friedrich Nietzsche*, Oscar Levy (ed.), were published by Macmillan, New York: 1909–1913. The Modern Library Giant, *The Philosophy of Nietzsche*, contains *Thus Spake Zarathustra, Beyond Good and Evil, Geneology of Morals, Ecce Homo* (a good autobiographical insight), and *The Birth of Tragedy*. The Mentor paperback, *The Philosophy of Nietzsche*, Geoffrey Clive (ed.), contains selections from the 18 volume Levy translation. Cf. "History," pp. 217–257. Karl Löwith has the best English language treatment of Nietzsche's cycle theory in his *Meaning in History*, pp. 214–222. It originally appeared in the *Journal of the History of Ideas*, VI (June, 1945), pp. 273–282. Nietzsche's *The Use and Abuse of History* is available in the Bobbs-Merrill Library of Liberal Arts paperback (1957). For a study of the cultural climate in which Nietzsche wrote, see Karl Löwith, *From Hegel to Nietzsche: The Revolution in Nineteenth-Century Thought* (New York: Doubleday, 1964). Cf. also J. Gaultier, "Nietzsche et l'idée du retour éternel," *Mercure de France*, CCXXVII (May, 1931), pp. 513–548. Nietzsche says simply in *The Will to Power*: "I have found this idea (of eternal recurrence) in earlier writers," namely, Heraclitus, Empedocles, Plato, and the Stoics.

of the ancient Greek for whom repetition on classical patterns was a criterion of an historical act's permanent significance. Nietzsche felt horror and awe that the historical process had no end, yet he felt that it was a joyful wisdom to absolutize time itself in its recurrent patterns. In his *Ecce Homo* (1888), he states that the eternal recurrence of all things is the fundamental idea of his work, the "highest of all possible formulae of a yea-saying philosophy." His unreliable sister, Elizabeth Förster-Nietzsche, tells us that her brother, as early as August, 1881, had resolved to reveal the teaching of eternal recurrence "in dithyrambic and psalmodic form, through the mouth of Zarathustra." [3]

Nietzsche's historical thought is significant because of the fact that it represents not only the most important revival of cyclicism in the modern world but also inasmuch as it stands as a formidable opponent to both Christian linearism and what Nietzsche considered its "trivialization," nineteenth-century progressivism.[4]

Nietzsche sees man as able to reconcile the conflict between freedom and necessity only by reaching beyond himself to the point of the "Overman," the superior individual whom Zarathustra proclaims to be the meaning of the earth. The Overman exultantly accepts the cosmos as it is, affirms finitism and rejects both secular and religious futurism. One cannot understand

[3] Cf. *The Philosophy of Nietzsche* (New York: Modern Library, n.d.), xxv. Nietzsche says in *Ecce Homo*: "Among my writings, my Zarathustra holds a special place. With it, I gave my fellow-men the greatest gift that has ever been bestowed upon them." *Ibid.*, p. 813. As a matter of fact, Nietzsche had really dealt with the problem as early as 1862 in two student essays, "Fate and History," and "The Freedom of the Will and Fate." Cf. Löwith, *op. cit.*, p. 214; and Walter Kaufmann, *Nietzsche, Philosopher, Psychologist, Anti-Christ* (New York: Meridian, 1956). Kaufmann, in the best appraisal of this theme in English, notes that Nietzsche did not believe that events themselves recur, and specifically repudiated the Pythagorean doctrine of recurrence (pp. 274–275).

[4] Nietzsche says in *The Anti-Christ*: "Mankind does not represent a development toward a better, stronger, or higher type, in the sense in which this is supposed to occur today. 'Progress' is merely a modern idea—that is to say a false idea" (Geoffrey Clive edition), p. 257. Cf. George Morgan's reference to the theme of progress in Nietzsche in *What Nietzsche Means* (New York: Harper and Row, 1965), p. 322.

Nietzsche's doctrine of recurrence without considering the companion doctrine of the Overman, which makes the former meaningful.

Nietzsche's historical outlook is conditioned by several factors, the first of which is his repudiation of any absolutist philosophy. His basic philosophic outlook is a fieristic monism—that is, an interpretation of reality as consecutive development of sheer becoming. In his *Genealogy of Morals* he attacks the notion of any "objective" truth or value, a concept he considers as reprehensible as the Christian conception of God, Hegelian absolutism, or Platonic metaphysics.

There is no lord of history and no goal of history as such; neither is there redemption in technological progress. Nietzsche's atheism is an instinctive repudiation of an absolute being based upon his conviction that religion is the result of the need for psychological compensation and ancestor worship; that worship constitutes a reprehensible draining off of vital human energies —an idea derived from Schopenhauer; that a beneficent God could not possibly tolerate the evil and misery of the existent world.

Nietzsche's position is also dictated by what Professor Collins has called the "psychologizing of the problem of God."[5] The phrase "God is dead," the message of Zarathustra, is not the proclamation of the death of a being who once lived, but the proclamation of the death of the *idea* of God in the mind of a humanity that is really worshipful of sensuality, wealth, and power. Whether or not one agrees completely with Morgan's contention that the major premise of Nietzsche's philosophy is atheism,[6] one must recognize that Nietzsche, in the parable of the madman (*The Gay Science*), does seem strangely aware of the apocalyptic emptiness of a world without God.

The consequence of the fact that neither God, nor an abso-

---

[5] Cf. James Collins, A *History of Modern European Philosophy* (Milwaukee: The Bruce Publishing Company, 1954), p. 786.

[6] Morgan, *op. cit.*, p. 36.

lutist system of truth and values, nor a teleological universe exists is that man must make his world, his values, and his history by giving shape to becoming. Having accepted the ultimate reality of change, he posits a kind of linearism not to the advancement of the species, but to the production of the aristocratic man—the *Übermensch* or Overman, who will not be subject to the pedestrian values of the vulgar masses, but who will be history's instrument of the Will to Power.

The Overman is not a totalitarian individual but an aristocratic type, a class that is challenged to overreach itself and to give future shape to the Will to Power. The Overman is not to be bound by the petty rules of the "slave" morality of Christianity, but represents the ascending line of human existence. He is the new Dionysius of vigorous, exploitative power, modified but not restrained by Apollinian intellectuality. He moves beyond the conventional good and evil to forge the values of a new moral existence and to reach an extramoral ethic, even though the ordinary man will live out his life on the lower plateaus of mass values.

The Will to Power is the great unifying element of Nietzsche's philosophy. He says succinctly in *Beyond Good and Evil*, "Life is precisely Will to Power," and identifies Will to Power as "the fundamental fact of all history." [7] As Nietzsche watched Prussian soldiers pressing forward to battle in the War of 1870, he was suddenly struck with the thought that life at its best is a fight for power. Power is the primal life force which shapes, uses, and exploits those external circumstances, the importance of which Darwin overestimates. [8]

The primal power of life tends to assert itself in a quasi teleology of selective growth even though lesser existences are destroyed in the process. Life is a going forward, a self-overcoming, a creating beyond oneself.

[7] *Beyond Good and Evil* (Modern Library ed.), #259, p. 578.
[8] Cf. George A. Morgan, *op. cit.*, Ch. III, "The Will to Power," pp. 59–83; and Walter Kaufmann, *Nietzsche, Philosopher, Psychologist, Anti-Christ*, Part III, "Nietzsche's Philosophy of Power," pp. 182–287.

History, then, becomes the record of this assertive drive for mastery over life's materials, whether it be masked as a desire for freedom, independence, organization, or control. Respect is not due to the individual as such, but only to the creative individuals. "The Overman is the meaning of the earth." [9]

In his *The Use and Abuse of History* (*Untimely Considerations*, Part II), Nietzsche brings out specifically his idea of history. It has, of course, nothing to do with the Hegelian idea of the rational unfolding of an absolute idea. History is necessary to man in three ways: in relation to his involvement in the world's concerns; in relation to his conservative reverence for the past; and in relation to his hopes for future deliverance. These three relations have reference to three kinds of history—monumental, antiquarian, and critical. Monumental is the idealized, heroic, and didactic analysis of the past; antiquarian, the archaist preoccupation with the past as dissociated from the present and future; and critical, a sober and analytic corrective by which the distortions of monumental and antiquarian history are remedied and reality is seen in focus. But the historical vision itself must be supplemented by the superhistorical, a vision of the as yet unrealized potentialities of man.

In effect, Nietzsche attempts to chart a world in which becoming assumes repetitive configurations shaped by will chiefly in the instrumentality of aristocratic individuals. The values are relative to the historical period which produces them, and although beings have evolutionary or developmental characteristics, there is no goal or purpose as such to which individual or corrective activity is directed.

When history degenerates into mere knowledge, it becomes for Nietzsche an antivital force dissociated from total human involvement. He resents the banishment of instinct by intellectualized history, as a result of which men are reduced to shadows

[9] "The great majority of men have no right to life, and are only a misfortune to their higher fellows." Levy (ed.), XV, 311, Aph. 872. Cf. also The Prologue to *Thus Spake Zarathustra* (Modern Library ed.), pp. 3–20.

or abstractions. History must serve the practical purpose of teaching man how to live.[10]

Nietzsche, however, saw the essential problem of history and stated it clearly. Is the model of human existence the classic one of eternally recurrent existence, or is it the Christian vision of the world as a creation of a God in whom man is to find—after his historical sojourn—his eternal happiness? Does the great clock of being constitute the diary of absolutized time, or is time more properly measured by a stationary hour glass whose sand grains gather eventually in a cumulative mass?

Nietzsche, of course, chose the former explanation. Changing nature powered by life is all, and history is but the record of the recurring peregrinations of its greatest figures.

DANILEVSKY

Preparatory to a treatment of Oswald Spengler, one should consider a writer whose interest at first sight seems far removed from both Spengler and cyclical history.

Nicolai Danilevsky (1822–1885), botanist, economist, political scientist, fisheries specialist, and ardent Slavophile, in the course of analyzing the supposed historical cultural animosity of Europe toward Russia, arrives at a general philosophy of history. That is, in seeking to understand the origin, duration, and future of historical conflicts between Russia and the West, he is led to a consideration of the historical problem as a whole.[11]

[10] Nietzsche opens *The Use and Abuse of History* with a quotation from Goethe: "I hate everything that merely instructs me without increasing or directly quickening my activity."

[11] A full bibliography of Danilevsky's works was published in Russian; Nicolai Danilevsky, *Political and Economic Essays* (St. Petersburg: 1890), pp. 673–676. His classic work, *Russia and Europe*, unfortunately is not available in English. A German translation, *Russland und Europa*, by K. Nötzell was published in Berlin in 1920. A good summary of Danilevsky's work is found in Pitirim A. Sorokin, *Modern Historical and Social Philosophies* (New York: Dover, 1963), pp. 49–71. Cf. also H. Stuart Hughes, *Spengler* (New York: 1952), pp. 44–50.

He identifies Europe not as a geographical entity, but as a cultural-historical unit of Germano-Roman civilization—one of many civilizations. Danilevsky considers European egocentrism to be based on erroneous assumptions concerning the nature of culture itself, the illusion of linearism, and the supposedly non-progressive character of non-European civilizations. He anticipates Spengler's criticism of periodization of history into ancient, medieval, modern, recognizing such a linear technique as a completely unrealistic analysis of the rich and repetitive character of historical experience.

History is not one movement seen from the vantage point of the European West; rather it is a multiple and repetitive movement of diverse tendencies and peoples.

Idealism as a distinguished tradition or thought style was indeed a highly complex cultural phenomenon that inevitably had its influence in the analysis of historical experience. Yet it is obvious that idealism was not a system or a philosophy in itself; like the empiricism it has traditionally opposed it represented a mood rather than a repertoire of specific convictions.

Idealism answered the need to unify experience in manageable thought patterns, and the synthesis produced by the idealist tradition tended to an over-all historical evaluation that assigned primacy to the world of thought and spirit.

The positivist tradition with its own orientation of particularistic analysis has modified idealism with a more sober regard for the concrete facts which make accurate generalization possible. But it has never replaced the fundamental idealistic conviction that reality is primarily an experience of non-tangible realities.

Danilevsky sees each historico-cultural form as exhibiting a process of growth analogous to that of organic development. And although each civilization has its unique character, the quasi-biological form of growth and decay remains. Thus, historical division consists in recognizing the different socio-cultural types.

The great civilizations of the world are the Egyptian, Chinese, Ancient Semitic, Hindu, Iranian, Hebrew, Greek, Roman, Arabian, and European, and two abortive types, the Mexican and Peruvian.

Besides the positive historico-cultural types, there are "negative agencies" in history (catalysts in the collapse of dying civilizations), and abortive societies referred to by Danilevsky as "ethnographic material," which are inorganic intrusions in historical organisms capable of no significant influence, either positive or negative.

Civilizations sometimes degenerate to the level of ethnographic material until a new creative integrating principle absorbs them into a new socio-cultural pattern.

Within the framework of these three types (historico-cultural types, negative agencies, and ethnographic material), Danilevsky analyzes world cultures with a view to formulating laws applicable to social phenomena. As a skilled botanist, he was particularly adept in utilizing the ideas and idioms of natural science.

Law 1. Every tribe or family of peoples identified by a language or by a group of languages whose resemblance is perceived directly, without deep philosophical explorations, constitutes an original historico-cultural type if it is mentally or spiritually capable of historical development and has already outgrown its childhood.

Law 2. It is necessary that a people enjoy political independence if its potential civilization is to be actually born and developed.

Law 3. The basic principles of a civilization of one historico-cultural type are not transmissible to the peoples of another historico-cultural type. Each type creates its own civilization under the greater or lesser influence of alien—preceding or synchronous—civilizations.

Law 4. A civilization of a given historico-cultural type reaches its fullness, variety, and richness only when its "ethnographic material" is diverse and when these ethnographic elements are not swallowed by one body politic, but enjoy independence and make up a federation or political system of states.

Law 5. The course of development of historico-cultural types is similar to the life-course of those perennials whose period of growth lasts indefinitely, but whose period of blossoming and fruitbearing is relatively short and exhausts them once and for all.[12]

As Spengler, Toynbee, and Sorokin after him were to affirm, each culture eventually exhausts its creative potentialities—its blossoming period being the relatively short period of from four to six hundred years—after the political unification of the people involved. It is the destiny of each historico-cultural type to realize some particular cultural value, as exemplified by the Greek beauty, European science, Semitic religion, Roman law and political organization, and Indian mysticism.

It is also characteristic of a civilization to seem to be at its most productive period when the process of decline has already set in. Although the precise nature of organic disintegration is not known, it is an internal rather than an external process.

There is a kind of special progress of which humanity is capable when a group of linguistically related civilizations exhibit a common influence in philosophy, religion, and the fine arts.

A final prophetic note in Danilevsky is his theory of cultural interpenetration; that is, not only the humanistic disciplines but the empirical sciences bear the mark of common cultural characteristics.

It is rather irrelevant to his more important theorizing that Danilevsky posits the questionable thesis that the Slavic-historico-cultural type is emerging as the first great synthesis of political, economic, religious, aesthetic, and technological cultural forces.

SPENGLER

Perhaps no modern figure has done more to revive interest in the modern world in a speculative philosophy of history than the

[12] As translated in Sorokin, *op. cit.*, p. 60. Danilevsky would seem to modify Law 3 by distinguishing solitary civilizations from successive or transmissible ones "whose fruits of activity were transmitted from one to another as material for nourishment, or as fertilizer (for enrichment and assimilation) for the soil on which successive civilizations would develop."

controversial Oswald Spengler (1880–1936), author of *The Decline of the West*.[13]

He is accused by the distinguished archeologist, William Foxwell Albright, of writing a work "fanciful and arbitrary to the highest degree . . . a curious blend of Hegelian philosophy and Goethean romanticism."[14] Henri Marrou even less kindly refers to Spengler's "mad lucubrations,"[15] and Erich Brandenburg speaks of his method as a "wild, reckless, uncontrolled construction of hypotheses."[16] Hughes recognizes the *Decline* as "a massive stumbling block in the path of true knowledge."[17] In 1922 the German scholar, Manfred Schroeter, wrote a book, *The Spengler Controversy (Der Streit um Spengler)*, a qualified defense of Spengler's intuitive method and a record of the earlier phases of the controversy.

Spengler's *Decline* represents a rejection of traditional ancient, medieval, and modern linear history of man, the rational animal, or mankind in general. Intuition, the brilliant insight, replaces rational analysis as a method of investigation. His purpose,

[13] *The Decline of the West*, trans. by Charles F. Atkinson, (New York: Knopf, 1926–28), 2 vols. The Helmut Werner Modern Library Giant (G 92) version is an abridgment, as is E. F. Dakin's *Today and Destiny*, published in 1940. The best study of Spengler in English is H. Stuart Hughes' *Oswald Spengler: A Critical Estimate* (New York: Charles Scribner's Sons, 1952). Cf. also Pitirim Sorokin, *Modern Historical and Social Philosophies*, Ch. IV, pp. 72–112, Ch. XII, pp. 205–243; R. G. Collingwood, "Oswald Spengler and the Theory of Historical Cycles," *Antiquity*, I (September, 1927), pp. 311–325, reprinted in *Essays in the Philosophy of History* (Austin, Texas: University of Texas Press, 1965), pp. 57–76, and a shorter critique in *The Idea of History* (Oxford: Oxford University Press, 1950), pp. 181–183. Collingwood considers Spengler's approach as "radically unsound." James T. Shotwell, "Spengler" in *Essays in Intellectual History Dedicated to James Harvey Robinson* (New York: Harper, 1929), pp. 55–67. André Fauconnet's *Un philosophe allemand contemporain: Oswald Spengler* (Paris: 1925), and Eduard Meyer's *Spenglers Untergang des Abendlandes* (Berlin: 1925), to the best of this writer's knowledge have not been translated. Cf. also Robert E. MacMaster, "Danilevsky and Spengler: A New Interpretation," *Journal of Modern History*, Vol. XXVI (June, 1954), pp. 154–161; and M. Braun, "Bury, Spengler, and the New Spenglerians," *History Today*, Vol. VII (August, 1957), pp. 524–529.

[14] William Foxwell Albright, *From the Stone Age to Christianity* (2nd ed. New York: Doubleday, 1957), p. 91.

[15] Marrou, *op. cit.*, p. 181.

[16] Erich Brandenburg, "Spengler's Untergang des Abendlandes," *Historische Vierteljahrschrift*, Vol. XX, 1 Heft, 1920, p. 18.

[17] Hughes, *op. cit.*, p. 1.

openly prophetic, is to predict "the spiritual form, duration, rhythm, meaning, and product of the still unaccomplished stages of our western history," to reconstruct from cultural data in the arts, politics, economics, religion, and science the organic character of entire centuries of history.[18] The narrower goal is the diagnostic one of explaining the specific decline of the western way of life as the inevitable phase of organic cultural degeneration. Negatively, the *Decline* is a protest against rationalism and, specifically, against linear progressivism. All cultures, according to Spengler, have a common morphological pattern of growth, development, and decline; and all cultural developments fulfill themselves and die down contemporaneously in all cultures.[19] A culture develops on the soil of an "exactly definable landscape," actualizes the sum of its possibilities, hardens into the shell of a civilization, and finally dies.[20] Cultures, for Spengler, are not *like* organisms, they *are* organisms, and world history is their collective biography. The idea of a culture is the totality of its possibilities, and each developmental stage is intrinsically necessary and temporally determined. The history of the world as a comparative study of morphologically determined cultures is consequently relativistic and prophetic; relativistic, in that all standards of truth, morality, and aesthetics are evaluated solely in terms of the culture in which they are found; prophetic, in that the gnostic intuitive vision of the superior historical mind has but to see what point of development the cultural organism has reached before knowing what has been and what will be.[21]

[18] *Decline*, I, p. 112. He ridicules the progressivist historian who fails to see history as the waxing and waning of organic forms and considers it a kind of tapeworm that keeps adding on to itself. *Ibid.*, I, p. 22.

[19] "I see, in place of that empty figment of one linear history which can only be kept up by shutting one's eyes to the overwhelming multitude of the facts, the drama of a number of mighty cultures, each springing with primitive strength from the soil of a mother region to which it remains firmly bound throughout its whole life cycle; each stamping its material, its mankind, in its own image; each having its own idea, its own passion, its own life, will, and feelings, its own death." *Decline*, I, p. 21.

[20] *Ibid.*, I, pp. 104–108.

[21] *Ibid.*, I, pp. 23, 25, 39, 47 for relativism. Spengler felt that what was missing until his time was a detachment from objects (*die Distanz vom Gegenstande*) considered necessary for objective appraisal of the historical process.

Spengler, who somewhat immodestly characterizes his work as "the philosophy of our time," never doubted that he possessed such gnostic insight.

His approach is fundamentally Goethean in that he depends on insight and feeling rather than on rational analysis, and anti-personalistic in that destiny rather than human causality is the regulative factor in history.

Cultures are identified by Spengler as Magian (Asiatic, including Christianity and Eastern European culture) which glorify science, Apollonian (classical Greco-Roman) which glorify reason, and Faustian (Germanic) which glorifies sensate Westernism.

Each culture has its own all-pervading value principle by which every element of that culture is affected. This, in a sense, is the key to the culture in question, or what Kroeber calls Spengler's "master pattern." It involves basic attitudes in thought and life and is best recognized in the plastic arts, music, and above all, in architecture. It begins in barbarism, elaborates itself in political structure, flourishes, becomes a sclerosed culture (civilization), as has been indicated, and eventually dies. The great cultures of the world have been eight in number: Egyptian, Babylonian, Indic, Chinese, Mayan, classical, Arabian, and Western. Arrested cultures such as those of the Hittites and Persians never achieve maturity. Spengler uses the term "pseudomorphosis," to refer to the stifling influence exerted by an older predominant culture on a young culture striving to articulate itself.

In his metaphysics, Spengler, who had written his doctoral thesis on Heraclitus, was a philosopher of becoming.[22] Change

[22] He was not, however, a skilled philosopher in any sense. Despite his indebtedness to Nietzsche, he remarkably misinterprets Nietzsche's historical thought as linearism (I, p. 24), has a rather bizarre appreciation of Plato's idealism (I, p. 49), and considers Scholasticism as exhausting itself with *Kant* (I, p. 365). Collingwood observes: "He consistently attributes to the Stoics the fundamental conception of the Epicureans . . . and he commits the appalling blunder of asserting that for Descartes the soul is in space. . . ." "Oswald Spengler and Historical Cycles," *op. cit.*, p. 61.

is characteristic of organisms, but it is a rigorously definable change. Curiously, Spengler is enamored of the biological imagery that Darwinism had made popular in the nineteenth century, but he balked at the "trivial optimism" of Darwinian progressivism. Even the repetition in successive cultures are "homologous" rather than identically recurrent. That is, there is a structural correspondence between the old and the new cycles that does not demand identical recurrence of events or entities. Spengler emphasizes, however, that it is unscientific to talk of mere likeness in describing homologous historical entities. An historical morphology must grasp the homology or correspondence of elements which allows for particular differences within a basic structural identity.[23]

A further word might be said about Spengler's method. He eulogizes Goethe and Nietzsche as his masters, supposedly deriving his questioning faculty from Nietzsche, and his noetic "insight" from Goethe whom he reveres, not only for his intuitional approach to knowledge and for his method of perceiving disparate realities in a vast total changing context, but also for his theory of understanding reality by a correct reading of its most meaningful symbols. Historical events are such symbols, and they inevitably reveal the latent reality of which they are but surface manifestations.

Like any determinist, whether theological, economic, or biological, Spengler minimizes the role of the individual, though he believes that every significant individual being necessarily "recapitulates" all of the epochs of the culture to which it belongs. In a system which is basically a comparative morphology of culture, it is the total living organism, not the individual person, which is historically significant. Likewise, it is historical destiny, not individually "caused" human acts, which is history making.

---

[23] Spengler uses the biological term, homology, to indicate morphological equivalence as opposed to analogy which he considers a functional equivalence. Cf. *Decline*, I, p. 111.

As the individual does not "cause" history, neither does he, unless he is one of the exceptionally gifted few, have the capacity for instinctively grasping the meaning of historical events.[24]

Spengler's narrower purpose of describing the situation of the cultural decline of the West begins with the birth of the Faustian world in the tenth century and concerns itself specifically with the gradual process of decline, the "civilization" phase of which begins in the nineteenth century. Creativity has been exhausted, and the degenerative process that Toynbee is later to describe as schism in the soul takes place. There is a lack of unity and a conflict of values. The political structure itself will fall to the power of finance; rival military groups will strive for power in a new Caesarism; a uniformly drab, mechanistic world society, uninspired and directionless, will continue to exist and seek meaning once again in a quasi-superstitious religious mystery. Primitivism will have come full circle.

Spengler found it difficult to understand the sensibilities of those who considered his work pessimistic, since he pictured himself merely the diagnostician of an inevitable cultural illness that individual striving is powerless to prevent. But he did address himself effectively to the somber mood of post-war Germany.

Spengler's popularity was destined to be relatively short-lived. His cynicism concerning democracy and popular socialism was foreign to liberalizing cultural aspirations; his somber predictions of decline were oppressively pessimistic to the Nazi mystique—however anxious Spengler was earlier to have his work allied with the military accomplishments of Germany, "the last nation of the West." Hughes perhaps best describes the dilemma of Spengler who was too scholarly to appeal to the political masses, and too imaginative and unscientific to appeal to the academicians.[25]

---

[24] This unique "feel" for the unity and significance of historical events, which Spengler identifies as his "physiognomic" method, is contrasted with the systematic or rational method of traditional history, which he feels to be not only unproductive but an obstacle to historical vision. Cf. *Decline*, I, p. 151. As Hughes observes, Spengler, in working out his "contemporaneity" tables, utilizes the systematic approach he supposedly condemns. Cf. Hughes, *op. cit.*

[25] Hughes, *op. cit.*, pp. 116–117.

The various criticisms that have been lodged against him (aside from those already cited) are: an inability to appreciate democratic theory; a naive conception of economics; a distorted and inadequate knowledge of Eastern culture; a robust certainty in highly questionable matters; an inflexible biological determinism; an anthropological ignorance of the nature of primitive societies; an archaic admiration for a vanishing social and military aristocracy; a manipulation of historical material to fit in arbitrary frames; and above all, a theory of the discontinuity of cultures. All these must be recognized as formidable objections. But Spengler did bring a larger unitary vision to historical events that was to influence a post-war generation of scholars. Like Vico, who was often mistaken, he brings an historical style, adapted to the realities of his era, that permits both correction and adaptation, and to a great degree an appreciation of the forces that go to make up the modern world.

Sorokin

Among one of the most provocative writers to present a theistic cyclicism is the Russian born sociologist and philosopher of culture, Pitirim A. Sorokin (1889–1968). Sorokin was very much involved in his world, having served as a secretary to Kerensky despite his "persistent apprehensions" about the Russian Revolution, and having at least twice been under the sentence of death for supposed political intrigue.

He came to the University of Minnesota in 1921, and became head of the Department of Sociology at Harvard in 1931 where he served as the Director of the Center for Creative Altruism.

Sorokin finds the chief clue to the mystery of history in culture change, and his fame rests principally upon his analysis of the socio-cultural systems "whose varying fates provide the very subject matter for the history of man and civilization." [26]

[26] T. R. Cowell, *History, Civilization and Culture: An Introduction to the Historical and Social Thought of Pitirim A. Sorokin* (Boston: Beacon, 1952).

His work has concentrated on the nature and cause of such changes based upon a thorough study of the arts, sciences, and social and political institutions of the cultures in question.

Sorokin's main thesis is to be found in the four volume *Social and Cultural Dynamics* and in the highly popular single volume (which Sorokin insisted was not an abridgment), *The Crisis of Our Age*.[27]

One might study Sorokin by analyzing in succession his descriptions of historical change, the nature of culture, and the great socio-cultural ideational, idealistic, and sensate systems.

Tertullian once referred to man as "naturally Christian" (*"homo naturaliter Christianus"*). Sorokin considers man as naturally historical, inasmuch as he feels it natural that man should not only want to be entertained and enlightened by the stories of the past, but that he should also want to know the overall significance of the events in question.

History always starts with contemporary inquiry, but questions lead one back into distant pasts, where actors are often dim shadows who steal but fleetingly into the sunlight where their acts may be clearly seen and understood. And no matter how detached or pragmatic the motivation of the inquirer, he cannot help but wonder what everything adds up to. The fact that reason asks the questions suggests that the human inquirer is not content with "unreason" as an answer. The search for meaning is perhaps a greater clue to the human dimension of the enterprise than the meanings eventually reached.

Like Spengler and Toynbee, Sorokin feels that what is needed to understand historical development is a change in the way of

---

[27] *Social and Cultural Dynamics* (New York: Bedminster, 1937), 4 vols., and *The Crisis of Our Age* (New York: Dutton, 1941). Included in his voluminous writings are the following books: *The Sociology of Revolution* (Philadelphia: Lippincott, 1925); *Contemporary Sociological Theories* (New York: Harper, 1928); *Sociocultural Causality, Space, Time* (Durham, North Carolina: University of North Carolina Press, 1943); *Russia and the United States* (New York: Dutton, 1944); *The Reconstruction of Humanity* (Boston: Beacon, 1948); *Social Philosophies of an Age of Crisis* (Boston: Beacon, 1952). The last volume was reissued in a Dover paperback in 1963 under the title, *Modern Historical and Social Theories*.

looking at history itself, especially a change from the progressivistic egocentrism that would have us believe that we of today
are the supreme accomplishment of all that has gone before.

Change may be occasioned by external or internal factors
within a culture. The first theory considers environmental factors and historical personalities within a perspective of a mechanistic or naturalistic philosophy in such a way that the agent is
more of a reactor to the various stimuli of his environment.

Immanentism would look for the answer to change within
the dynamism of the system itself and accord to external conditions a minimum influence. The vitality of cultural life in any
specific area will thus be dependent upon cultural vitality as a
whole. Organic conceptions such as Spengler's would illustrate
this kind of immanentism.

A third answer to the problem is found in a combination of
both external and immanent factors, a solution that Sorokin
seems to feel is often artificial and forced, and one that is often
not sufficiently integrated to constitute a real solution to the
problem.

Sorokin himself believes that change is basically from within,
but admits the possibility that external factors may exert a
limited moderating influence. A socio-cultural system will either
change or achieve the dubious equilibrium of stagnation. A
change is a law of life; the explanation for change must be found
within the life process of culture itself, and it is to be remembered that the external environment itself is composed of changing systems.

The life span of a culture will reflect the innate potentialities
of the culture itself rather than some invariable morphological
pattern; and external factors may indeed inhibit, retard, or accelerate the realization of cultural potentialities, particularly at an
early period of its existence.

Sorokin admits that a cultural system, though structurally
determined to a general mode of fulfillment, may well admit of
variant possibilities in the curve of its development and of conclusions dependent on the vagaries of free choice. The self-

determination of any system will depend on the degree to which it is integrated, that is, to the degree to which the system can command the physical environment and influence human behavior.

A culture will have greater power and self-control if its members are biologically, mentally, and morally superior; such a culture will have greater organization because it is based on wisdom and knowledge. There will be recurrent rhythms within every socio-cultural system, but identically recurrent systems are impossible.

In other words, Sorokin rejects a strictly cyclical recurrence theory in just the same way as he rejects unmodified linearism.[28] Growth exists certainly, and so also does recurrence. But these will always be conditioned by the accumulated experience of the socio-cultural system in general.

Retardation, progress, and regression undeniably exist. But there would also seem to be justification for concluding that there are recurrence patterns based on three distinctive types of socio-cultural systems, each of which is valid and adequate to a limited degree.

These three systems he identifies as "ideational," "idealistic," and "sensate." An ideational culture is an age of faith when spiritual values and the reality of the divine and the supersensory predominate. It glorifies asceticism and discipline and other-worldliness in general. A sensate culture is based on a preoccupation with science, the natural order, and its values alone. It emphasizes sensual pleasure, is preoccupied with the grandiose, exotic, and erotic. It emphasizes the changing, relative aspects of being and rejects the supernatural. An idealistic culture represents a synthesis of these two opposing socio-cultural systems, recognizing the dynamism of spiritual qualities and the power of creative imagination working in the world. Idealism, in this sense, recognizes what is sound and best in the other two traditions, a balanced and harmonious culture whose "major premise

28 Cf. Cowell, op. cit., pp. 236–238.

is that the true reality is partly supersensory and partly sensory." [29]

He disagrees with Spengler in asserting that no cultural system wholly dies, although it is eventually substantially altered. Mankind is pictured as contributing to its destiny, especially through its few creative individuals who give shape and dimension to an age by what he calls "creative altruism."

He feels the time propitious to a new idealistic age when man's greatest human potentialities may be realized.

Sorokin is perhaps arbitrarily classified as a cyclicist; but it is true that he does give striking new emphasis to recurrent elements in contemporary cultures without reducing such elements to cyclic determinism.

SUGGESTED READINGS

NIETZSCHE

Friedrich Nietzsche, *The Use and Abuse of History, trans. Adrian Collins, Indianapolis: Bobbs-Merrill, 1957.

Crane Brinton, Nietzsche, New York: Harper and Row, 1965, Ch. IX: "Nietzsche in Western Thought: Prophecy on a Prophet," pp. 232–243.

Geoffrey Clive (ed.), The Philosophy of Nietzsche, New York: New American Library, 1965, Ch. V: "History," pp. 217–257. (Selections from the eighteen-volume Oscar Levy translation. Topical arrangement from Karl Schlechta's new German edition.)

Walter Kaufmann, *Nietzsche, Philosopher, Psychologist, Anti-Christ, New York: Meridian, 1965, Ch. XI: "Overman and Eternal Recurrence," pp. 266–287.

Karl Löwith, "Nietzsche's Doctrine of Eternal Recurrence," Journal of the History of Ideas, VI (June, 1945), pp. 273–282; *Meaning in History, Chicago: University of Chicago Press, 1949, pp. 214–222.

George A. Morgan, *What Nietzsche Means, New York: Harper and Row, 1965, Ch. III: "The Will to Power," pp. 60–83; Ch. XI: "Dionysios," pp. 291–318; Ch. XII: "The Rise and Fall of Cultures," pp. 319–350.

[29] Sorokin, The Crisis of Our Age, p. 20. This highly readable book reveals Sorokin's conviction that the value principle of every culture penetrates its systems of thought, arts, science, and religion. Like Spengler, Sorokin approaches this problem from the starting point of contemporary crisis, seeing the chaos of the hour in the light of the decay of the sensate system. Cf. Cairns, op. cit., p. 379.

SPENGLER

Oswald Spengler, *The Decline of the West*, trans. by Charles Francis
    Atkinson, New York: Knopf, 1957, I: pp. 3–50.
H. Stuart Hughes, *Spengler, A Critical Estimate*, Ch. V: "The Decline:
    The Morphology of Culture," pp. 65–88.
Pitirim A. Sorokin, *Modern Historical and Social Theories*, New York:
    Dover, 1963, Ch. XII: "A Critical Examination of the Theories of
    Danilevsky, Spengler, and Toynbee," pp. 205–243.

CHAPTER SEVEN

IDEALISM AND HEGELIANISM

When Hegel delivered his lectures on the philosophy of history in 1822, he was not inaugurating a new style of thought but continuing a century-old tradition that was a blend of romanticism and idealism. The newer trend might be generally described as preoccupation with person and idea rather than with system and formalization, with the subjective rather than with the objective.[1] And yet Hegel by no means ignored the so-called objective dimension of human existence and certainly brought systematic formalizing to a new dimension.

The German tradition of idealism differed markedly from the formal empiricism of the English and French traditions, much in the same fashion that the Anglo-Saxon preoccupation with linguistic philosophy today differs markedly from the continental

[1] We shall be concerned here primarily with the last section of Hegel's philosophy of Logic, Nature, and Concrete Spirit. This section treats Subjective Spirit (anthropology, phenomenology, consciousness), Objective Spirit (right, morality, ethical life, the state), and Absolute Spirit (art, religion, and philosophy). It must be remembered that students rather than Hegel himself are responsible for the publication of courses in the philosophy of history, esthetics, philosophy of religion, and the history of philosophy. Cf. the complete outline of Hegel's system in the end fold-out of W. T. Stace, *The Philosophy of Hegel* (New York: Dover, 1955)—a relatively brief and clear exposition of Hegel's thought, to the degree that Hegel's thought is amenable to brief and clear exposition. For an excellent introduction to Hegel cf. Walter Kaufmann, *Hegel: A Reinterpretation* (New York: Doubleday, 1966).

interest in the existentialist and phenomenological philosophical traditions.

It is relatively easy to understand idealism in history as some kind of a subjective reenactment of the past; it is more difficult to understand how what seems to be irretrievably lost *can* be recaptured by one who, to a very limited degree, can project himself into the alien world of the past. A man can, if he is reasonably articulate, express what he might feel as a pilgrim into the past; but he is simply not in a position to *be* that man in the past, possessed of no oracular knowledge of events with which the historian is already familiar. The historian is like a man seeing a mystery film for the second time; he cannot in simulated innocence possibly pretend the second time around that he does not know that the butler is the culprit.

Hegel's *Phenomenology of Mind* (1807) is a synthesis of early writings on the evolution of consciousness and ideology. Hegel's *Encyclopedia of the Philosophical Sciences* (1817) provides a broad view of his system; *The Philosophy of Right* (1821), a systematization of his social and political views.

Idealism in its essence is the belief that actuality is more closely associated with thought and idea than with the world of things perceived by the senses. It is an orientation rather than a specific philosophy which makes the experiencing subject indispensable to any consideration of objectivity itself.[2] If thought is primary, then history is primarily the record of a fundamentally subjective process. If, on the other hand, the positivist is correct in his conviction that reality is reducible to the dimensive and quantitative, then history is strongly going to be influenced by natural science and its development. But if what is real is rational, and what is rational is real, as Hegel maintained, then the objective and subjective worlds are not really separated. The focal point of idealism in the late eighteenth and nineteenth centuries was the problem of the scientific character of history.

[2] Cf. Talcott Parsons' excellent chapter, "The Idealistic Tradition," in *Structure of Social Action* (New York: McGraw-Hill, 1937), pp. 473–499.

Scientific method was a blend of rational inquiry and empirical testing, but there was an increasing conviction in the German academic community in the late eighteenth century that scientific method was inadequate to meaningful historical inquiry.

HEGEL

G. W. F. Hegel (1770–1831) is significant to the philosopher of history because, despite his idealistic monism, his highly implicative philosophy raises history to a new dimension, and has, in fact, influenced almost every significant political ideology since his time.[3] His system he sees as the fulfillment of philosophical consciousness that begins especially with the primacy of thought in Aristotle and moves through his own time in the incomplete contemporaneous thought styles of Fichte and Schelling.

At the outset of the lectures that were to make up his *Philosophy of History*, Hegel distinguishes original, reflective, and philosophical history. The first is the mental representation of deeds, events, and conditions of society by observers of the time. Reflective history is an attempt to gain a comprehensive view of a people, a country, or the world; it is universal, pragmatic, critical, or fragmentary. Philosophical history is a thoughtful consideration of the Absolute in its varying and successive forms.

Hegel's thought is not a linearism that would represent history as having realized itself in the Prussian State. The ultimate reality, Absolute Spirit, reaches a significant point of consciousness in the Prussian State of Hegel's time, but the highest historical realization is not terminated there. A given state represents a divine totality of all the artistic, religious, and cultural forces within it, a visible purpose reflecting the All, but not equivalent

---

[3] Not all writers are happy about this influence. Cf. Karl R. Popper, *The Open Society and its Enemies* (New York: Dover, 1966), Vol. II, pp. 27–80. Popper quotes Schopenhauer as calling Hegel's influence "stupefying" and "pestiferous." *Ibid.*, p. 80.

to the All. Each state, the Prussian included, represents a phase of Idea. World history is the succession of these phases.

Nations grow and die, but in dying on the poisoned fruit of fulfillment (the image is Hegel's), they set the stage for a new nation and a new people. One cannot understand history at all, according to Hegel, unless one sees the endless variety and changing forms of political life.

History is in a sense the diary of the Absolute, as progressive freedom and consciousness is worked out in time; it is also inevitably a philosophy of history in that history is neither a mere philosophically oriented reflection on the past, nor a scientific compilation of fact patterns, but a universal developing consciousness which concretizes but does not confine or exhaust itself in the political state.

There is a newness and a uniqueness in the historical event, although there is an ordered progression of Spirit in the world to self-comprehending totality. The Absolute as Spirit (Geist) has been called Hegel's greatest conviction as well as the major premise of his thought. Included in the concept of *Geist* are the appetitive and cognitive powers, the passions, the physical world, as well as more obviously spiritual realities. Spirit is substance in the sense that it signifies a self-conscious content of a real self that undergoes progressive development to an ordered "self-becoming." It is thought in that it is reflective consciousness and science or philosophy itself.

Mind progresses historically through Oriental, Greek, Roman, and Germanic-Christian phases, which correspond to the ages of historical life from childhood to old age. In the first era only the ruler is free; in classical times only some are free; and in the modern world "man as man is free."

There is, however, a kind of dualism in Hegel in that history is the development of Absolute Spirit in time, as Nature is the development of Idea in space. Idea-in-itself is primal reality, the antithesis of which is Idea-outside-of-itself, or Nature. Hegel's monism thus resolves the apparent dichotomy between mind and matter by recognizing man, the agent in history, as a developmental phase of Nature in which Idea rises to the level of consciousness. Spirit represents the resolved antithesis between Idea and Nature, and the biography of this Spirit constitutes history.[4]

Although Spirit through the cultural influence of Christianity (and especially, according to Hegel, Protestant Christianity) emphasizes the spiritual and transcendent character of God, Spirit is not exhausted by religion's concept of the Ultimate (God), and Hegel is particularly critical of the remote, transcendent, polarized God of traditional theism.

For Hegel the development of the Absolute in time is destined in a special way through ethical consciousness to the production of the political state in successive organic phases. The state is distinguished from its temporal and finite manifestation in a *particular* state, as has been noted. Hegel recognizes the inevitability of discordant elements in the state and the need of corrective and cooperative adjustments of conflicting groups within society.[5] Individual man sees his need filled and overreached, as it were, by the state, whose coercive power is necessary to effect harmony. The pragmatic adaptation made by men in a specific environment is reason at work in individual men in their personal and corporate decisions.

[4] Hegel, *Reason in History*, trans. by Robert S. Hartman (Library of Liberal Arts, #35; Indianapolis: Bobbs-Merrill), pp. xxi–xxv. The entirety of Professor Hartman's valuable introduction is recommended. This work, originally given as prefatory lectures in the philosophy of history by Hegel, is based on *Die Vernunft in der Geschichte*, but is not an exact translation of it. Cf. also R. G. Collingwood, *The Idea of History* (Oxford: Oxford University Press, 1946), pp. 113–126. Hegel's idea of the role of consciousness in the historical process is best treated in the difficult volume previously referred to, *Phenomenology of Mind* (1807), Harper Torchbook edition, 1967. Consciousness is treated both as a study of human knowing in its development and as a cause of specific ideologies.

[5] Cf. Hegel's *Philosophy of Right*, trans. by T. M. Knox (Oxford: Oxford University Press, 1942); James Collins, *A History of Modern European Philosophy* (Milwaukee: The Bruce Publishing Company, 1954), p. 647. The entire section on Hegel in Collins (pp. 600–661) is recommended, as well as the same author's *God in Modern Philosophy* (Chicago: Henry Regnery, 1954), Ch. VII, "God and the Hegelian Absolute," pp. 201–237.

The state as politically realized is the ultimate synthesis of Objective Spirit, the dialectical product of family and civil society; but the synthesis which is the state points to a higher purpose, the cultivation of art, religion, and philosophy. If one can possibly ascribe a goal to history in the Hegelian synthesis (other than to cite such elusive phrases as the eternal conscious self-realization of Absolute Spirit), that goal might indeed be the development of art, religion, and philosophy within the framework of the state. For art, religion, and philosophy represent the greatest thrust of Absolute Spirit in grasping the same ultimate reality in differing scaled modes of representation. Art reveals the ultimate in the idiom of the sensuous and the concrete. Religion uses the idiom of the symbolic and the sensuous, but is found wanting by Hegel in differentiating God and man, the supernatural and the natural. In philosophy alone pictorial imagery, feelings, and insight are superseded, or rather fulfilled, by authentic understanding.

The state, however, has a great value in the Hegelian synthesis besides providing the soil for the progressive development that culminates in the philosophical vision of the Absolute. It is considered the ultimate actuality of the ethical idea, and consequently the objective manifestation of the divine idea, because it represents the form in which individual free men and their social, religious, and artistic institutions can develop. It actualizes man's freedom.

But the Hegelian state is a strong state with plenary control over its members who are served by their subservience to the larger encompassing whole. Allied to this latent totalitarianism is Hegel's failure to develop any theory of a meaningful international coalition of world states, and his acceptance of war as an instrument of national policy.[6]

---

[6] There would seem to be in Hegel's thought a philosophical objection to a supreme international arbiter or world court. The judgment on nations is decreed by Absolute Reason alone, rather than by arbitrary legal judgment against "divine" states, and the sovereign power of the individual state has no superior juridical limit.

Hegel's theory of life as divine totality involves a radical re-viewing of traditional theism. Finite mind reflecting upon itself sees itself as related to complete actuality. The reflective human consciousness is Absolute Spirit rather than a product of Absolute Spirit.

The philosopher of history may not be convinced by Hegel's denial that he is a pantheist, and pantheism may indeed be an oversimplification of his thought, since the All is divine only in a highly ambiguous sense. The God of history is not denied, although in a sense he is by-passed in favor of an immanent self-developing process, a monism of Absolute Spirit. The Idea-in-itself *is* God before creation, and it is in the fulfillment of creation that God is known. God might be said to be the Absolute in the religious phase of triadic development; and he might be "dead" in the sense that one proceeds through pro-gressive dialectical rationalization from religion to the clearer and philosophical appraisal of the ultimate.[7] Hegel, like Nietzsche after him, believed that divine transcendence as held by the Jewish and Christian traditions induces an unhappy master-slave relationship, and he refused to recognize any finite dimen-sion of existence that is not contained by the infinite. To accept a transcendent God is to degrade man.

Quite obviously, this is not a "death of God" in an older atheistic sense, but an approach to ultimate reality in what is felt to be a more meaningful idiom. Hegel's objection to tradi-tional theism was based on his conviction that it was a distortion and objectifying of the Absolute. Even in his early *Positivity of the Christian Religion* (1796), he lamented the objectivization of God "put into another world in whose confines we had no part, to which we contributed nothing by our activity, but into which, at best, we could beg or conjure our way." [8]

---

[7] God for Hegel is also "dead" in the sense of ceasing to elicit belief in the Western world. He has become removed, abstract, and unreal for modern man. Cf. *Reason in History*, pp. 16–19.

[8] *The Positivity of the Christian Religion* in *Early Theological Writings*, trans. by T. M. Knox and R. Kroner (Chicago: University of Chicago Press, 1948), pp. 162–163.

It is to be noted that Hegel has had a great, if unacknowledged, influence on contemporary theologians, although paradoxically, they are similarly indebted to Kierkegaard who is a savage critic of what he feels to be the impersonal, cosmetically neat and rational system of Hegel.[9]

Freedom enters very much into the Hegelian concept of history, as the essence of Spirit itself is freedom. History is the march of freedom through the world, and this march is the progressive aspiration, realization, and concretization of Absolute Spirit in the world. Hegel seems to consider freedom as an undeveloped Idea which articulates itself progressively in external social and political institutions.

He considers it superficial to view the history of the world in terms of needs, talents, and passions of individual men, although he concedes their legitimacy. "The individual is," as W. T. Stace says, "implicitly universal . . . the state is the actual universal, and is thus simply the individual actualized and objectified." [10] All individual activities, however independent they may seem, are instruments by means of which Absolute Spirit assumes divinized political expression through what Hegel calls "the cunning of Reason." The realized purposes of individual wills serve a larger purpose of which the particular agents are unaware. As Reason governs the world, it governs the world's history.

[9] When the now famous Bishop Robinson discussed what he meant by "ultimate reality" in his article, "Our Image of God Must Go," in the London Observer of March 17, 1963, he sounded more like Hegel than Bonhoeffer preaching a "religionless Christianity." And the late Paul Tillich preferred to speak of God as "the ultimate concern," "the very ground of our being," "the deepest springs of our historical existence," "the depth of experience interpreted by love." Rudolf Bultmann argues that the gospel must be demythologized of its prescientific cosmology and concepts, among which is the spatial notion of transcendence. Paul Van Buren argues that as secular men we must present a Christian message without the language of metaphysics or the term God. William Hamilton pictures himself as waiting and hoping for a God who may be dead to rise up again. Leslie Dewart and Harvey Cox question the necessity of Christianity's retention of the name God to refer to ultimate reality on grounds which are basically Hegelian. Cf. Walter Kaufmann, *Hegel, A Reinterpretation (New York: Doubleday, 1966), pp. 274–275.

[10] W. T. Stace, op. cit., p. 425.

Of particular importance are "world historical individuals" whose significance consists chiefly in the effective pursuit of aims that coincide with Absolute Spirit. They are heroic individuals, not by reason of the detached brilliance of their exploits, but inasmuch as the source of their action is a concealed fount of a larger wisdom.[11] They are blessed with a particular insight for the needs of their time and are usually blessed with a practical political expertise that deservedly makes them the leaders of their time.

Hegel, for instance, sees Napoleon as the soul of the world who sees the need of his historical moment, establishes necessary sovereignty, and reconciles individual aspirations to the larger needs of a stable political system. Hegel makes it quite clear that individual and state are not equivalent contracting parties. The state alone is the objective and necessary entity.

But although Spirit is the inmost soul of leaders, theirs is not the lot of serene accomplishment. They are committed to the labor and conflict of unhappy creativity, and are destined to stir their world and die without even the solace of the larger vision to which their lives were perhaps inadvertently dedicated.[12]

One of the reasons Kierkegaard was so outraged at Hegel was the latter's calm acceptance of misery and evil as necessary dialectical moments in the historical life of Spirit, although Hegel never denies the existence of irrational elements in the world. He touchingly refers to the world's misery and avers that our thoughts cannot avoid contemplating for whom and for what final aim "monstrous" sacrifices have been made.[13] Hegel falls easily back into his Lutheran vocabulary—he strangely relapses into a Christian idiom despite his heterodox notions of transcendence and his obvious monism—to describe the history of

[11] Hegel, *Reason in History*, pp. 39–43.
[12] Hegel adds to the proverb, "No man is a hero to his valet-de-chambre"— "but not because the former is no hero, but because the latter is a valet."
[13] Hegel, *Reason in History*, pp. 26–27.

the world as God's governance. God *is* self-realizing Reason.[14]

Hegel draws a fairly conventional distinction between the study of natural organic existences and those acts which are the products of a self-determining rational consciousness. History can never be a blind organic process, although it exhibits the characteristics of biological growth and development in the waxing and waning of human institutions.

He indicates further the possibility for individuality and progress that arises from the dialectical nature of Idea, which strives to overreach itself and metamorphose into richer external existences. The peculiar style that arises from the dialectic interplay of mind and specific environment is an "idiosyncrasy of Spirit," a national genius, that marks every aspect of life from art to science and religion, and gives each state its distinctive characteristics.

Hegel's is not a comparative study of equivalent cultures, although the life cycles are similar. Each state is judged in terms of its adequacy to the state of consciousness to which mankind has come. Changes in the natural world exhibit only a "self-repeating cycle," whereas historical change brings progressive enrichment.[15]

Sabine interestingly observes that Hegel's theory of the state gave impetus both to the conservative tradition of the national state as the embodiment of political power and the dialectic

[14] Cf. Hegel on religion in *Phenomenology of Mind*, pp. 683–786. Hegel, however, despite his early Lutheranism and the influence he exerted on contemporary theologians, was not a Christian. His Christianity is a methodological convenience in understanding truths which can better be understood by philosophy. English excerpts from A. Kojève, *Introduction à la lecture de Hegel* (Paris: 1947), are to be found in Cornelio Fabro, *God in Exile: Modern Atheism* (New York: Newman Press, 1968). Kojève says: "There is of course no question here of a mystical union and the term God is here nothing more than a metaphor. There is no Being to Whom (or Which) the philosopher unites himself for he *is* total Being: and he is 'God' only in the sense that the Whole of *his* Knowing (Knowledge) which is the Whole of truth, is but a development of the *sum qui sum* . . . the Knowledge he has of his being *is* his very Being." p. 623. Cf. also Emil L. Fackenheim, *The Religious Dimension in Hegel's Thought* (Indianapolis, Indiana: Bobbs-Merrill, 1968).

[15] *Philosophy of History*, p. 54.

"which provided the starting point for a new proletarian radicalism." [16]

In fine, all that is real is rational; all that is rational is real. Philosophy is the highest mode of knowledge, the ultimate in self-reflective reason. It is philosophy which evaluates the role of the historical realization of the Absolute, and in this sense, Hegel's philosophy of history is really the history of philosophy. For philosophy alone gives that special insight which enables man to understand that portion of knowledge which we know as history. Morris Cohen has called Hegel the greatest philosopher of the nineteenth century, and few can doubt his influence, direct or indirect, on the twentieth century mind.[17] An unsympathetic critic once observed that Hegel's vast system was so neat and beautiful because at no point did it come into contact with reality. It would seem much closer to the truth to acknowledge with Hans Rosenberg that Hegel's is a great synthesis, not only because of its encyclopedic universalism and the architectonic marvel of its structure, but by reason of its richness and influence on the contemporary world. One wonders, on contemplating Hegel, Vico, and Spengler, not that they accomplished so little, but that they dared so much.

DILTHEY

Of less importance than Hegel, but a man whose importance in cultural history has been underestimated, is Wilhelm Dilthey (1833–1911). Influenced by von Ranke at the University of Berlin, Dilthey abandoned early plans to study for the ministry in favor of philosophy and history. His intellectual curiosity also led him into critical studies in literature and music, educa-

[16] George H. Sabine, A History of Political Theory (New York: Holt, 1950), p. 623.

[17] Carl J. Friedrich, The Philosophy of Hegel (New York: Modern Library, 1954), p. xvi.

tion, social thought, and religious history, which were to aid him in the synthesis of historical reason on which he spent a half century of his academic career. Hodges observes that Dilthey, like Vico, Hegel, Croce, and Collingwood, drew his inspiration from history and aesthetics rather than from the empirical sciences.[18]

Dilthey was concerned about the disproportionate influence of the mathematical sciences in the cultural history of man, although he granted the legitimacy and desirability of exact knowledge when obtainable. But man, the object of historical study, is a much more elusive subject. Lost in the complexities of a cultural past and given to whimsical personal decision, he is not subject to experimentally verifiable laws. Dilthey's aim was not only to stress the importance of the humanitarian disciplines as equally worthy of study as the sciences of nature, but to see what the coordination of those former sciences could yield in the way of overall knowledge.

Dilthey is important to the philosopher of history because he asks the same questions but is strongly critical of traditional answers. He does not believe in a philosophy of history if, by philosophy of history, one means a speculative attempt to find ultimate meaning in the course of historical events.[19] Nor is he ready to yield an inch to the pretensions of positivism and scientism. But he was interested in the enormously important question of psychological motivation in what was practically a prepsychological age.[20] Like Nietzsche, who considered the doctrine of progress a secularized creationism, Dilthey considers

---

[18] H. A. Hodges, *The Philosophy of Wilhelm Dilthey*, London: Routledge and Kegan Paul, 1952), p. xiii. Cf. also Volume VII of the Teubner edition of his eleven-volume *Gesammelte Schriften* (Leipzig: 1924). The German biography by Otto Bollnow has not, to this author's knowledge, been translated.

[19] "Dilthey's philosophy is not a philosophy of history if that means a theory of historical thinking as such. It is a *philosophy of understanding*, and because it is, it is also a *philosophy of culture* . . . History is a vehicle of understanding. It is 'life embracing life.' " *Ibid.*, p. 319.

[20] Cf. *Psychoanalysis and History*, Bruce Mazlish (ed.) (Englewood Cliffs, New Jersey: Prentice-Hall, 1963).

philosophies of histories as interpretative efforts which arise when a theology of history dies. Dilthey, in a sense, is interested in history as reflective of a deeper interest in the basis of all knowledge and the reason why we posit the great metaphysical questions of human existence.

Man's quest he sees as only partly intellectual. It is the whole man who is immersed in life and seeks to intuit its meaning. Life for Dilthey is not mere animal vitality, but the richness of experienced existence in which the person acts and reacts to his world. Dilthey is impatient with the formal thinker or academician who would reduce that richness to an intellectual system.[21]

Dilthey published his *Introduction to the Sciences of Mind* about a decade before his younger contemporaries, Windelband, Rickert, and Simmel published works of similar nature. Although his projected masterwork, *Critique of Historical Reason*, was never written, Dilthey did write on the theory of history in shorter works; he poses the problem of the legitimacy of historical knowledge by questioning the possibility of data to reveal the reality of which they are the manifestations. Historical knowledge must somehow be a psychologically experienced situation in which the facts of the past are incorporated into the larger understanding.

The psychologizing of historical knowledge creates its own problems, chief among which is the validity of knowledge of events not immediate to the knower. It is not the past event

[21] German contemporaries of Dilthey particularly interested in the Nature vs. History theme were Simmel, Windelband, and Rickert, the latter two of whom were in frequent controversy with Dilthey. Windelband, in 1894, stressed the character of science as a search for the universal, and history as an "idiographic" knowledge of the individual events on which man makes ethical value judgments. Rickert objected that nature, too, is built on facts as well as laws derived from them, but did not stress the developmental or causal character of their relationship. Simmel rejected the exclusivity of empirical science as knowledge, stressing the intimate personal reconstruction of human situations in the mind of the historian as the desirable methodology. The importance of this idealist tendency in late nineteenth-century thought was to reject Schopenhauer's dour judgment that history was not scientific, and to establish historical inquiry as a search for a vision of the past not limited to factual minutiae.

that is experienced, but the event as preserved in the historian's consciousness; and this subjective experience does not automatically justify the objectivity of the content experienced.

It must be admitted, however, that history was but one of the human studies (*Geisteswissenschaften*) that Dilthey wished to preserve against the forces of positivism and skepticism which threatened the validity of nonempirical sciences.

He does attempt to give structure to historical thought, but he is always motivated by this larger aim in behalf of the humanities. Man does not impose this vision on life, but he tends to see human life in terms of a worldview, a historical consciousness.

There is perhaps too great a tendency to associate Dilthey exclusively with the idealist tradition, first of all because of his Hegelian interest in synthesizing knowledge, and because of the stress he places on the psychological states of the historical inquirer.

But Dilthey's conclusions are not dictated by eternal truths or principles aprioristically adopted. The thought structure itself arises from the psycho-physical being's relationship with his actual world, and reminds one that Dilthey never seems to avoid the empiricism he would deny as the sole source of knowledge.

He has a Kantian's disdain for metaphysical answers, but a Kantian's respect for metaphysical questions—which he attempts to answer from the totality of man's intellectual, volitional, and emotional experience. He has a great, if not exclusive, interest in the history of that experience, but no interest in an abstract rationalist synthesis, as reflected by the fragmentary character of his writings.

Although history is but one of the *Geisteswissenschaften*, its role is unique in that it alone transcends the limited life-experience of lesser inquiries to see life in its totality.[22]

[22] This is not to say that any particular *Weltanschauung* captures the full significance of life; but unless one has the overall vision of historical consciousness, he cannot understand a given philosophical development. Cf. William Kluback, *Wilhelm Dilthey's Philosophy of History* (New York: Columbia University Press, 1956), pp. viii–ix.

Dilthey also places considerable importance in the historical inquirer's ability to intuit the characteristic spirit of a given period—a methodology of romanticism that was to become famous in Spengler. Like Hegel, Dilthey was a monist, and both the capacity for intuitive understanding and desire for synthesis are perhaps reflective of a pantheistic worldview he had from his youth.[23]

Of particular interest is the evolution of Dilthey as a theorist on history. It has already been noted that one of the main preoccupations of Dilthey, Simmel, Windelband, and Rickert was the historical concern for the development of an authentic methodology for the non-empirical sciences of human society.

G. P. Gooch has observed that before the nineteenth-century historical thought suffered from a rationalist contempt for the medieval period, an absence of basic collections of archival sources and a critical technique for handling such materials, and the lack of a systematic approach to the study of either content or method.[24] Romanticism strangely enough served as a corrective to rationalist narrowness, but it is similarly strange that the romanticists, even while they struggled to free themselves from the mathematical orientation which is the ordered rationalist's passion, tried to give the *Geisteswissenschaften* a foundation that simulated mathematical accuracy.

The interesting thing is not that this was ever successfully accomplished (for it was not), but that it was attempted. The attempt to find an objectivity comparable to that of the material sciences was at once an inadvertent tribute to empirical science's

---

[23] Dilthey studied at Heidelberg under Kuno Fischer, to whom he is indebted for his knowledge of philosophy's most significant personalities. He was also influenced by Hölderlin, Hegel's closest friend and one of Germany's most famous poets; and by Schleiermacher, one of nineteenth century Germany's most famous theologians. Informal seminars at the homes of Adolf Trendelenburg and Moritz Lazarus made him conversant with the latest thinking in theology, philosophy, literature, music, art, social and political thought.

[24] G. P. Gooch, *History and Historians in the Nineteenth Century* (Boston: Barnes and Noble, 1962), pp. 11–12. Gooch, in speaking of Friedrich Meinecke, says: "No German scholar since Dilthey, whose stature has been recognized by the collection in twelve volumes of his penetrating essays, has analyzed ideologies with such insight and subtlety." p. xiii.

contribution to knowledge and a vigorous critique of its methodological insufficiencies.

Part of the greatness of von Ranke was his investigation not only of the authenticity of historical materials but also of the personality of the historian as well as the integrating spirit of age or nation that would enable the dispassionate inquirer of later ages to describe things as they actually were—"*wie es eigentlich gewesen.*"

Like Vico, who pointed to more doors than he opened, von Ranke never developed the synthesis of economic, artistic, social, and political history that would best identify this *Zeitgeist*. But he developed in a long career the academic seminar technique by means of which the larger questions could be effectively approached by his students.

Dilthey's is a significant contribution to the widening historical curiosity that would replace political history and quasi-mechanical fact gathering with a truly intellectual history. That this type of history has at times produced a forced polarization is true; that this type of inquiry has yielded rich insights and has many descriptive advantages is also true.

Specifically, Dilthey envisioned the historian in a practical as well as theoretical role. Aware of the continuity of culture in succeeding generations, the historian sees uniquely the genesis and survival of values and should strive for those political and social goals his knowledge reveals as desirable. Ideas grow out of experience as well as from reason; that is, history itself produces ideas. Dilthey follows Kant in accepting the need of establishing critical norms for knowledge and in the latter's rejection of traditional metaphysics, but he considers Kantian man too intellectualized and too far removed from the actual milieu in which he lives.

Dilthey follows neither Kant nor Hegel in his rejection of man as the rational animal. His interest in psychology made him realize that there is much in man that is not rationally motivated, yet he never despaired of establishing his idealism on a realistic foundation that would take into account the emotional, the cognitive, and the volitional in the historical life of man. The spiritual dimension of human existence he realized could not be adequately described by the manipulative symbols of mathematics. The nonhuman sciences culminate in laws, but the humanities produce values, and it is on values that an historical worldview depends. But it is not life as a speculative value, but life as lived that is history. As Dilthey points out: "History is only life comprehended from the point of view of all mankind, built into a unity." [25]

In Dilthey we have the repeated emphasis, later to be found in Ortega y Gasset, that history is not a speculative academic enterprise, but the vital interaction of human beings in a given environment.[26]

Dilthey's pantheism differs markedly from the idealistic monism of Hegel. In the "universal-historical continuum," life assumes temporal forms and configurations in a never-ending historical sequence. Professor Kluback observes:

> The union of the life-philosophy and the evolutionary pantheism was the basis of Dilthey's view of the historical process. Man, by nature, had to express himself. Those expressions that were recorded formed the universal historical stream. . . . Man engaged, then, in a continual process of taking from the stream of history, refining the contents in terms of his own interests, and giving the refined product back to the stream.[27]

The idea is significant in history because it is generated by the vital contact of man in his environment. It is permanent in that it is part of an enduring human nature, but temporary in that it is produced at a given moment in time.

[25] *Gesammelte Schriften*, Vol. VII, p. 256.
[26] Ceplecha observes: "Ortega shared Dilthey's wish to complete Kant by writing a critique of vital and historical reason. . . . The dialogue between the ego and the circumstance is history. . . ." *The Historical Thought of José Ortega y Gasset* (Washington, D.C.: The Catholic University of America Press, 1958), p. 161. Cf. also Ortega's "Guillermo Dilthey y la idea de la vida," *Obras*, Vol. VI, pp. 198–199. Ortega has a passage similar to Dilthey's quoted above: "Only our life has meaning in itself. . . . Our life is the universal interpreter." *Ibid.*, Vol. VI, p. 385.
[27] Kluback, *op. cit.*, p. 57.

Like Molière's Monsieur Jourdain, who was surprised that he had been speaking prose all of his life, Dilthey, the enemy of metaphysics, ends up with a metaphysics of becoming that assumes the form of historical relativism. The task of historically-situated man is to break, so to speak, into the reality of the historical world, by understanding the passing scene itself and the way in which the human mind is equipped to grasp it. Dilthey, like Goethe, Spengler, and Burkhardt, sees man understanding history by reading its objective symbols in architecture, art, literature, and social institutions. Goethe had said, "Everything transitory is only a symbol."

External reality reveals the ultimate in realities peculiar to a time and place, and the historian's task is to try to understand the integument of ideas constituting the historical consciousness that produces a given set of socio-cultural symbols. One proceeds progressively to understand the symbol, the system of ideas, and universal history itself.

Like Nietzsche, who felt that basic forms (*Grundformen*) as organically transmitted contain a recapitulation or a "remembering" of all that is past, and Schleiermacher, who felt that the universal experience of all men is contained in individual man, Dilthey was scrupulous in understanding the present in terms of the past.[28]

Dilthey's next step is to claim not only that a structure of historical continuity exists which can be known by the historical inquirer, but that the categories of the mind guarantee the validity and scientific character of the knowledge gained. In short, because of the universal similarity of the structure of mind, contemporary man, in grasping a portion of truth, can understand other minds at work in the same fashion.

From this process emerges a worldview which will assume the form of subjective idealism, naturalism, or objective idealism.[29] That is, the mind imposes its subjective forms upon reality,

[28] Cf. *Gesammelte Schriften*, Vol. V, p. 4. Nietzsche claimed that all organic functions are forms of the will to power.

[29] Cf. Kluback's excellent description of these world views, *op. cit.*, pp. 67–69; and Hodges, *op. cit.*, pp. 88–95.

passively reflects reality, or vitally reacts to external reality and modifies and is modified by it.

To know history, therefore, is to know the categories of mind interacting in a given environment, and the precise ideas arising out of the life-situation that will give rise to one of the basic worldviews. He has, in a sense, to relive the past creatively and reflectively. Like Hegel, who sees the state as a divinized soil producing the ultimate triad of art, religion, and philosophy, Dilthey sees man as developing in the specific environment of the state. The story of such development and objectivization is world history, and Dilthey reserved for history the ultimacy that Hegel reserved for philosophy.

Hughes sees Dilthey's and Croce's thought as effecting a veritable revolution in historical writing that has produced this historian's contemporary attitude to his craft.[30]

CROCE

Perhaps the most famous of contemporary idealists is Italy's greatest modern scholar, Benedetto Croce (1866–1952), who also repudiates the traditional, chronological view of historical knowledge in favor of a subjective reevaluation of the historical past. Croce's belief in human freedom precludes the possibility both of mechanistic repetition and history as prophecy.

When a relatively young man, Croce had concerned himself, in the tradition of Dilthey, with the problem of the nature of history that was such a controversial subject in late nineteenth-century Germany.

His first concern is with the problem of history as an art and as a science; since he considers art an intuitive grasp of being in its individuality, history, as a concern for facts, is essentially an art. He concedes the scientist's concern for facts, but insists

[30] H. Stuart Hughes, *History as Art and as Science* (New York: Harper and Row, 1964), p. 43. Hughes also credits von Ranke with effecting the earlier revolution which produced modern historical study in Germany.

that such concern is subordinated to the fashioning of general laws, a task utterly alien to the practicing historian. History is therefore identified with art, conceived not as a something merely representational or sensuous, but as a direct vision of individual reality that finds technical expression. He recognizes the particular need of history for an accuracy not demanded by the pictorial arts, but was later to expand his concept of history to include a cognitive as well as an intuitive dimension that would give to history an essentially philosophic quality.

Croce, like his German contemporaries, is interested in freeing history from the methodology of natural science, but rather than consider it vaguely as a science of a special kind, he refuses to recognize it as a science. Collingwood observes:

> Croce, by denying that history was a science at all, cut himself loose from naturalism, and set his face towards an idea of history as something radically different from nature . . . It was the clean cut which he made in 1893 between the idea of history and the idea of science that enabled him to develop the conception of history so much farther than any philosopher of his generation.[31]

There is a progressive development in Croce's thought as he grapples with the mystery of historical experience. His identity of art and history does not reveal how history's crucial concern for the real and unreal can be compared with the object of art, which, though individualized, does not have to be real or "truthful" in any literal sense.

He is eventually to identify a specific historical judgment as a combination of the individual and universal, inasmuch as the individual thing or event is grasped by universal concepts of a reflected process which is essentially philosophy.[32]

---

[31] Collingwood, *The Idea of History* (Oxford: Oxford University Press, 1946), p. 193.

[32] Croce was 43 when, in 1909 in his *Logic*, he expounded the role of philosophy in the historical judgment. Reality is historical, that is, it consists in universals (philosophy) articulated in specific facts. His *Aesthetic* was written in 1902, and *History, Its Theory and Practice* in 1916. This latter work was intended as Croce's final volume of his *Philosophy of the Spirit*, but is, as the author suggests, a deepening and amplification of his theory of historiography originally outlined in the *Logic*. *Ibid.*, p. 5.

He distinguishes the mental activity of science from that of history. Scientific concepts are pseudo-concepts, constructions that are helpful to us in dealing with nature. The historian, on the other hand, lives imaginatively in other persons at other times.

He believes himself capable of reconstructing the past by a rethinking in which he shares the reality of the past. Every true history must be contemporary history, because of the fact that the past finds its actuality in the present only through the activity of the existential mind. Croce felt that if it were not possible to get into the mind of the agent of the past, the best one could do was to assemble inert cultural remnants in some kind of order.

Croce, however, did not develop a philosophy of history from this noetic, but he did develop an important negative attitude toward the possibility of a philosophy of history. As history is not an empirical science, it is independent of science's manner of operation; as it is already philosophical, it is free of manipulative Hegelian master plans.[33]

Croce sees not only a basic opposition between a philosophy of history and historical determinism (the former a transcendental conception of the real, the latter an immanent), but also finds determinism incapable of generating a philosophy of history. He sees facts as brute things and the tendency to link them together in a chain of causation as largely fruitless. He criticizes Taine's naturalistic aphorism, "after collecting facts search for causes," because he feels that the inquirer often invests proximate causes with an ultimacy that they do not really possess.[34] The search for a transcendental end, which he considers the philosophy of history, is just as contradictory as a determinism which ignores human insights and interests, and reduces facts to codified events of nature.

[33] Croce considers history as a preface to science in that facts can not be organized into law until their historicity as facts are ascertained in the first place. *History, Its Theory and Practice*, Ch. IV, "Ideal Genesis and the Dissolution of the Philosophy of History," pp. 64–82.
[34] *Ibid.*, p. 65.

He not only considers the historian's search for a transcendental end an oversimplified one, but suggests that philosophies of history are, to a large degree, poetical replacements of facts for words and reality for images. He thus remains suspicious of a deterministic search for causes and a philosophical quest for "meaning" that he notes particularly in the work of Labriola, Simmel, and Rickert, and in the abortive efforts of Flint.[35] Both approaches he calls "futile," and identifies them as journeys "erratic" and "full of useless repetitions."

A more positive picture of Croce's theory is to be found in Chapters I and IX of *History, Its Theory and Practice*. First of all, as has been observed, he says of history that "the condition for its existence is that the deed of which history is told must vibrate in the soul of the historian." [36]

He observes that what we call "human history" also has a natural history; and what we call natural history presupposes a living "human history." If one cannot make oneself into a Sicilian neolithic man, one must content oneself with classifying and arranging skulls and utensils. If one cannot make oneself into a blade of grass in order to understand its history, one must content oneself with analyzing the parts and "disposing them in a kind of imaginative history." Unlike a Spengler, who was later to picture himself as rediscovering "long vanished and unknown" epochs as a paleontologist might reach trustworthy conclusions of skeletal structure from a single skull fragment, Croce sees a pseudo-history as limited in its revelation.[37]

History springs from life in that even an interest in past things springs from a present concern. In short, it is not the inert things of the past that constitute history, but a present thinking on past things. "Thing, not thought, is born of thing."

History, moreover, is living chronicle; chronicle is dead history, the detachment of mind from living reality. Croce, for this reason, refuses to consider chronicle as in any way prior to history. Chronicle is a mere effort of will to gather brute facts and prevent them from exposure to the present.

> The Romans and the Greeks lay in their sepulchres, until awakened at the Renaissance by the new maturity of the European spirit.[38]

The result of Croce's work was to reassert the independence and academic respectability of history as a separate enterprise against what were felt to be encroachments by both science and philosophy. A fact gatherer is not an historian, because he is lost in an impersonal world of things; but a romanticist who merely feels or throbs as a substitute for thinking may be a good poet but is most assuredly a bad historian. Both extremes of pseudo-history defile the past, for it is not enough for the historian to be mentally alive, but he must be mentally alive to actuality.

Suggested Readings

HEGEL AND HISTORY

G. W. F. Hegel, *The Philosophy of History*, trans. by J. Sibree, New York: Peter Smith, 1956, intr. by C. J. Friedrich. This translation is based on Karl Hegel's edition of 1840–43; *Reason in History*, trans. and intr. by Robert S. Hartman, Indianapolis: Bobbs-Merrill (Liberal Arts Paperback), 1953.

Bernard Bosanquet, *The Philosophical Theory of the State*, London: St. Martins, 1958, Ch. X: "Hegel's Philosophy of Right," pp. 238–274.

Louis Dupré, *The Philosophical Foundation of Marxism*, New York: Harcourt, 1966, pp. 3–66.

Walter Kaufmann, *Hegel, A Reinterpretation*, New York: Doubleday, 1966, Ch. VI, "Hegel on History," pp. 249–297. Kaufmann's section on Bibliography (pp. 371–394) is especially helpful in distinguishing authentic works from edited publication of classroom lectures.

Frank E. Manuel, *Shapes of Philosophical History*, Stanford, California: Stanford University Press, 1965, Ch. VI: "Leaps into Free Consciousness: Resonances from the German Academy," pp. 115–121.

Herbert Marcuse, *Reason and Revolution*, Boston: Beacon, 1960, Ch. VII: "The Philosophy of History," pp. 229–248.

[38] *History, Its Theory and Practice*, p. 24.

Friedrich Meinecke, *Machiavellism*, New York: Praeger, 1965, Ch. XIII: "Hegel," pp. 343–369.

George H. Sabine, *A History of Political Theory*, New York: Holt, 1950, pp. 620–667.

W. T. Stace, *The Philosophy of Hegel*, New York: Dover, 1955. Section III, The State, pp. 422–428; Sub-Section III, World History, p. 438; Third Division, Absolute Spirit, pp. 439–442.

DILTHEY AND HISTORY

H. A. Hodges, *The Philosophy of Wilhelm Dilthey*, London: Humanities, 1952.

Hajo Holborn, "Wilhelm Dilthey and the Critique of Historical Reason," *Journal of the History of Ideas*, XI (January, 1950).

H. Stuart Hughes, *Consciousness and Society*, New York: Knopf, 1958, Ch. VI: "Neo-Idealism in History," pp. 183–248.

William.Kluback, *Wilhelm Dilthey's Philosophy of History*, New York: Columbia University Press, 1956.

CROCE AND HISTORY

H. W. Carr, *The Philosophy of Benedetto Croce*, New York: Macmillan, 1927.

R. G. Collingwood, *The Idea of History*, Oxford: Oxford University Press, 1946, pp. 190–204. *Essays in the Philosophy of History*, Austin, Texas: University of Texas Press, 1956, Ch. I: "Croce's Philosophy of History," pp. 3–22.

Benedetto Croce, *History, Its Theory and Practice*, trans. Douglas Ainslie, New York: Russell, 1937. This work is especially helpful in its treatment of the historiography of the Renaissance, the Enlightenment, Romanticism, and Positivism.

S. Sprigge, *Benedetto Croce, Man and Thinker*, New Haven: Yale University Press, 1952.

CHAPTER EIGHT

TOYNBEE AND THE GOAL OF HISTORY

In March, 1947, a relatively little-known but much respected English historian by the name of Arnold Toynbee appeared on the covers of *Life* and *Time*, an accomplishment that is contemporary America's nearest approach to the bestowal of immortality.

Despite the fact that there existed at the time a small group of the historian's admirers who had gone painstakingly through six erudite volumes—they were later to become known as the "preabridgement Toynbeeans"—Mr. Toynbee became famous not only because of his own formidable talents, but because of a fellow historian's hobby.

The historian in question was D. C. Somervell, and he made an abridgment of Toynbee's six volumes without the latter's prior knowledge and without any intention of publication.[1]

Only when the project was finished was Mr. Toynbee informed of its existence, and happily acquiesced in its publication, having gone over the manuscript and having made appropriate additions and revisions.

Within weeks, a volume on the philosophy of history that spoke of such esoteric things as Thalassocracies and Hittite

[1] Cf. the author's "Toynbee and the Somervell Abridgments," *The American Ecclesiastical Review*, Vol. CXXXVII, 1, pp. 39–51.

culture was competing on the best seller lists with books dealing with more spirited, if less cerebral, adventures.

Like Spengler with whom he was often to be compared, Toynbee brought a massive erudition, a richness of allusion, and a fresh originality to the study of human culture; and he was similarly destined to endure the unpopularity of some of the more conservatively-oriented members of his profession.[2]

Specifically, Toynbee wrote six volumes of what Christopher Dawson calls "a relativist phenomenology of equivalent cultures."[3] After an interval of fifteen years, many of which were devoted to government service during the war, Toynbee wrote four more volumes changing his thesis to "a unitary philosophy of history comparable to that of the idealist philosophers of the nineteenth century."[4]

The formerly cyclic character of the early volumes yields to a linearism in which the higher religious and ultimately a syncretic faith became the goal of history.

Toynbee starts his work by considering societies, rather than nations or periods, the legitimate objects of historical study.[5]

[2] Despite many significant similarities to Spengler, Toynbee is not a believer in cultural morphology. Cf. *Civilization on Trial* (New York: Oxford University Press, 1948), p. 9; *A Study of History* (New York: Oxford University Press, 1963); Vol. I, p. 87; Vol. III, p. 383.

[3] Cf. Christopher Dawson "Toynbee's Odyssey of the West," *Commonweal*, October 27, 1954, p. 62. The volumes of A *Study of History* are: Vol. I: Introduction and the Geneses of Civilizations (1934, 1935); Vol. II: The Geneses of Civilizations (continued) (1934, 1935); Vol. III: The Growth of Civilizations (1934, 1935); Vol. IV: The Breakdown of Civilizations (1939); Vols. V and VI: The Disintegration of Civilizations (1939); Vol. VII: Universal States and Universal Churches (1954); Vol. VIII: Heroic Ages and Contacts between Civilizations in Space (1954); Vol. IX: Contacts between Civilizations in Time, Law and Freedom in History and the Prospects of Western Civilization (1954); Vol. X: The Inspiration of Historians, A Note on Chronology, Acknowledgments and Thanks, Index to Volumes VII–X (1954); Vol. XI, Vol. XII: Reconsiderations, A Reply to Critics (1961).

[4] Dawson, *op. cit.*

[5] The thesis is summarized in each of the Somervell abridgments as "Argument," pp. 567–589 (Vols. I–VI), pp. 355–393 (Vols. VII–X), 1947 and 1957 respectively. A bibliography of works on Toynbee from 1946–1960 by John C. Rule and Barbara Stevens Crosby is found in *History and Theory*, Vol. IV, 2 (1965), pp. 212–233. A brief critique of Toynbee's civilization categories is found in William Foxwell Albright, *From the Stone Age to Christianity* (New York: Doubleday, 1957), 96–102.

The world has seen twenty-one such societies and civilizations, fifteen of which are affiliated to previous civilizations and six of which have developed directly from a primitive stage.

All civilizations are evaluated in the organic terms of genesis, growth, breakdown, and disintegration, popularized earlier in a variant form by Spengler, but Toynbee rejects the concepts of race and environment in the progress of civilization, noting that there is no evidence of an innately superior race, nor any reason to believe that comfortable environments are conducive to cultural growth.

In the tradition of Dilthey he feels the inadequacy of empirical techniques in dealing with spiritual problems, and suggests that growth is to be understood, not in biological or geographic terms, but in terms of a formula of Challenge and Response. That is, a response to a quasi dialectic in nature: man is challenged by negativity to be creative. It is not the easy life, but such challenges as "hard countries," new ground, blows, pressures, and penalizations that drive a people to productive effort. He realizes, however, that a challenge can sometimes be overwhelming and render a civilization abortive; the maximum challenge will not always produce the optimum response.

In Volume Three Toynbee is concerned with the problem of civilization growth. He notes that a civilization does not grow as a matter of course once it has been brought into existence. A civilization might meet one challenge successfully and a consequent one badly. The arrested civilization of the Polynesians, Eskimos, Nomads, Osmanlis, and Spartans are such cases. Toynbee treats the subject of utopias in this section, seeing in the utopian dream a product of a civilization in decay. The utopia may either be a compensatory escape or a practical program to arrest deterioration.

Societies achieve growth neither by command over neighboring peoples in military conquest, nor in increasing technical command over the physical environment. The dedicated individual and creative minority are responsible for growth. The creative individual practices a "Withdrawal and Return" like a

St. Paul, Mohammed, St. Benedict, or Dante. He leaves the world for contemplation and enlightenment so that the world to which he eventually returns may profit from his creative absence.

A growth factor of singular importance to Toynbee is a law of progressive simplification which he more precisely identifies as "etherealization." That is, once the problems of the material medium are successfully solved, forces are liberated within society to deal with the great moral and spiritual challenges which present themselves.

Toynbee sees dynamic political minorities also as subsocieties capable of both withdrawal from the mainstream of the life of their respective societies and return to the progressive enrichment of their civilizations.

Different societies have characteristic religions, artistic or industrial talents, and though all share a common structure, they are not deterministically directed to a common fate.

Toynbee begins his analysis of the breakdown of civilization with the observation that of all the civilizations that have existed, only the Western, Far Eastern, Orthodox Christian, Islamic, and Hindu have survived. Breakdown occurs when the dynamism of the creative minority congeals into routine formalism; the creative minority becomes a dominant minority incapable of providing leadership; and the society itself loses its basic unity.

He regrets the deterministic solutions of those who would attribute breakdown to "cosmic senescence," organic decline (Spengler), and cyclicism, as well as the solution of Gibbon who would consider Christianity the debilitating cultural force.

Breakdown involves a loss of mimesis; that is, a voluntary follower who gives allegiance to a creative minority may no longer be inspired to follow. If the minority becomes dominant, it may force the individual to be a member of the proletariat, a subgroup wthin a society that does not share the large society's goals, and is in, but not of, the society in question.

Breakdown, therefore, involves a voluntary human factor, not historical inevitability. Old institutions are called upon to do new work. A wavering society seeks stability in idolizing an ephemeral self or institution or in suicidal militarism.

The culmination of the breakdown process is disintegration. There is widespread schism in both the body and soul of society in the consequent fragmentation of the civilization in question. The dominant minority characteristically tends to create a universal state, the internal proletariat a universal church, and the external proletariat, barbarian war bands. But the continued vitality of the Christian Church, from which Western culture was born, has prevented the production by the internal proletariat of a new "higher religion" in the contemporary world of the West.

The external, like the internal, proletariat comes into existence as a seceding segment of the dominant minority of a disintegrating civilization, and it is more physically separated from the parent culture.

Schism in the soul produces the alternate substitutes of abandon and self-control for creativity, truancy and martyrdom for discipleship, the sense of duty and the sense of sin for the vitality of growth.

It also engenders an archaism which provides escape into a secure and roseate past. It creates a futurism which, through expectation, anesthetizes one to the unpleasantness of the present, and a sense of promiscuity which manifests a progressive barbarism.

Of all the saviors who appear at the time of social disintegration—political or military saviors, archaists, futurists, and God incarnate in a man—only Jesus of Nazareth brings life.[6]

In Volume Six Toynbee investigates the problem of Universal States which are seen, not as ends in themselves, but as Indian summers of decadence, whose mission is to prepare the way for the "higher religions." Toynbee envisions the state, not in a

---

[6] Cyclic and spiral features of Toynbee's thought are treated by Grace E. Cairns, *Philosophies of History* (New York: Citadel, 1962), Part III, Ch. IV: "Cyclical Form of the Culture Pattern in Toynbee's Philosophy of History," pp. 403–455. Cf. also Toynbee's *An Historian's Approach to Religion*, p. 10; *A Study of History*, Vol. VI, pp. 235–236; and *Civilization on Trial*, p. 232.

divinized Hegelian sense, but as a cultural continuum capable of establishing order and uniformity among disparate people and territories.

THE "NEW" TOYNBEE

The "new" Toynbee appears in Volume Seven in the discussion of Universal Churches. No longer are universal churches secondary to civilizations as intelligible units of historical study; they are envisioned in their relation to the great extant religions of Christianity, Mahayana Buddhism, Hinduism, and Islam.

Later volumes concern themselves with rather diffuse and occasionally irrelevant divagations on the Heroic Ages, Contacts between Religions in Space and Time, Law and Freedom in History, The Prospects of Western Civilization, and Reconsiderations, a detailed response to various critics over the years.

Of particular importance is Toynbee's new conception of a syncretic faith as the end of history, which is more reflective of his compassion as a civilized man rather than his expertise as a theologian.[7]

Viewing, as does Spengler, the contemporary crisis of the West within the context of a larger aim of historical interpretation, Toynbee sees the present crisis as a response by Russia and the Orient to the multiple challenges of the West. Seeing the Western way of life as similar to that of the declining Roman empire, he pictures the West as possibly receptive to a new faith that

---

[7] Cf. Arnold Toynbee, An Historian's Approach to Religion (New York: Oxford University Press, 1956), and A Study of History, Vol. VII. Cf. also the author's "Arnold Toynbee and His Syncretic Faith" in Twentieth Century Thinkers, John K. Ryan (ed.), (New York: Alba House, 1964), pp. 213–220; Roger Shinn, "The Religious Vision of Arnold Toynbee," Christianity and Crisis, Vol. XV, pp. 43–46; Linus Walker, O.P., "Toynbee and Religion: A Catholic View," The Thomist, Vol. XVIII, pp. 292–299; and Edward Rochie Hardy, "The Historical Validity of Toynbee's Approach to Universal Churches," The Intent of Toynbee's History, Chicago: 1961, pp. 151–180.

will retain the Christian belief in a God of love, but will jettison dogmatic formulas and structures in favor of the more tolerant attitude of the East.[8]

No longer is civilization the most significant unit of study in Toynbee's thought. Religion is the end of civilization, which exists to promote it, although religion is seen as a basically evolutionary reality that progresses through a dialectical conflict of opposites. Thus, challenge and response remain as a basic rhythm of historical existence, although material progress is neither inevitable nor the ultimately desirable.

In a manner reminiscent of Bacon and Vico, Toynbee sees man as prone to worship idols in an attempt to stabilize a basically changing existence. The idols may be an institution, a creed, a person, or a state, but all are false concretizations of vital realities.

Toynbee resembles Hegel not only in his realization of the antithetical nature of reality, but in his rejection of supernatural revelation, miracles or prophecy, and traditional theism in favor of the Modernist concept of religion as an evolving human experience. Philosophies are merely cultural effluvia of their civilizations, and theologies represent at best verbal attempts to reconcile what are called scientific and prophetic truths. Toynbee recognizes no theory of the analogy of being, and consequently accuses theologians of anthropomorphism in conceiving of God in terms of feeling, will, and intellect.[9] Yet Toynbee inadvertently uses analogy in recognizing God as supreme being, and human love as an adumbration of the fullness of divine love.

Evolutionary religion has found expression in the contemporary world in the four extant "higher religions" previously referred to. Each of the faiths is not a divinely revealed religion, but an extrapolation of a basic psychological need. Christianity and Islam emphasize the reality of God as transcendent, and

---

[8] In the Oxford Galaxy paperback edition, the Volume on the Universal Churches is 7B, pp. 381–771 (successive pagination).

[9] *A Study of History*, Vol. 7B, pp. 467–468.

Hinduism and Buddhism emphasize divine immanence. Christianity, Judaism, and Islam are Judaic faiths; Hinduism, Hinayana and Mahayana Buddhism are all, for Toynbee, Buddhaic in inspiration.

Soon after their epiphany, the higher faiths succumb to the blandishments of power, by serving political interests; logic, by fashioning theologies; and self, by claiming uniqueness and ultimacy.

Religion itself is rejected by modern man in favor of Oecumenicalism, Nationalism, and Technology. Toynbee sees the oecumenical state as the sole survivor of these alternate visions for religion. But the oecumenical state in his vision of the future will bring security at the expense of precious freedom.[10] For instance, the worldwide welfare state he envisions would be forced, in the face of population crisis, to impose birth control on the world community. The "acute claustrophobia" produced by such regimentation will impel man to risk liberation in a realm of the spirit, in which the four extant religions will become aware of their mission to unite mankind in a four-part harmony.[11]

What is most interesting about this rather unusual excursion into the world of prophecy is not that Toynbee rather strangely ignores such very much alive religions as Judaism and Hinayana Buddhism, and oversimplifies them as immanent and transcendent, but that his entire thesis is ultimately dependent upon Jung's version of psychological need.

Toynbee pictures each higher religion and each of their sects as ministering to a psychic necessity. He sees the psyche's elemental needs incapable of being met by any one faith, and insists that no spiritual organ can play a "psychic diapason."

The divers higher religions must school themselves to playing limited parts, and must school themselves to playing these parts

---

[10] Cf. *An Historian's Approach to Religion* (New York: Oxford University Press, 1956), Ch. XVIII, "The Religious Outlook in a Twentieth Century World," pp. 239–253.

[11] Toynbee allows Mr. Martin Wight to state a Christian position by way of criticism in a special annex in 7B, p. 737.

in harmony, in order, between them, to fulfill their common purpose of enabling every human being of every psychological type to enter into communion with God, the Ultimate Reality.[12]

It would be inaccurate to classify Toynbee's work as a new Augustinianism. He indeed believes in a personal God, the dignity of man, and the freedom of the will; but it is difficult to see Christianity in Toynbee's thought as anything more than one distinctive vision of reality.

Toynbee's synthesis is a deeply felt, personal vision of the nature of religion and the meaning of history. But it would seem to be more accurately identified as a religious and linear rather than a specifically Christian view of history. Toynbee's own background is Christian, and the Christian idiom is present even when the Christian conviction is not. Toynbee would like to see a Christian-inspired reconciliation between hitherto "exclusive-minded religions" that would effect a unity of the world's peoples.

However laudable this aim, it is difficult to envisage both the possibility and the result of the fusion of the world faiths. One is faced with the initial difficulty of finding a common denominator among the four faiths themselves before attempting the impossible task of finding the ultimate syncretic faith that would indeed be history's most notable achievement.

However disenchanted one might be with the end result of Toynbee's quest, one can only be fascinated by the journey. Allan Nevins has said of him: "Standing on his Everest, he is more than a historian; he is a prophet." Prophets have always had a difficult life, and especially when they labor in a community of historians where the utterance of prophecy is suspect.

In summary, Toynbee, like Hegel, combines linear and cyclic elements in his thought. Civilization exists in a cycle of birth and death, and through their life and death man moves linearly to the knowledge and love of God.

[12] A *Study of History*, 7B, p. 734.

SUGGESTED READINGS

Arnold Toynbee, A *Study of History*, New York: Oxford University Press, 1963, Vol. 7B, *Universal Churches; An Historian's Approach to Religion*, New York: Oxford University Press, 1956; *Civilization on Trial*, New York: Meridian, 1936.

Christopher Dawson, *The Dynamics of World History*, New York: New American Library, 1956, "Arnold Toynbee and the Study of History," pp. 390–404.

Douglas Jerrold, *The Lie About the West*, New York: Sheed and Ward, 1954.

Edward Whiting Fox, "The Divine Dilemma of Arnold J. Toynbee," *The Virginia Quarterly Review*, Vol. XXXIX, 1, pp. 104–133. A review of *Reconsiderations* (Vol. XII) which is Toynbee's appraisal of the criticism directed at his work over the years. The two basic charges he considers are fact manipulation and the abandonment of scholarship for prophecy.

Edward Gargan (ed.), *The Intent of Toynbee's History*, Chicago: Loyola University Press, 1961. A cooperative appraisal by William H. McNeill, Friedrick Engel-Janosi, David M. Robinson, G. E. Grunebaum, Hans Kohn, Matthew A. Fitzsimmons, Edward Rochie Hardy, Eric Vogelin, Oscar Halecki.

Pieter Geyl, Arnold Toynbee, Pitirim A. Sorokin, *The Pattern of the Past: Can We Determine It?* Boston: Beacon Press, 1949.

Martin R. P. McGuire, "Toynbee's Study of History—Fruitful Failure on the Grand Scale," *The Catholic Historical Review*, Vol. XLII, pp. 332–329. An excellent short summary.

M. F. Ashley Montagu (ed.), *Toynbee and History: Critical Essays and Reviews*, New York: Sargant, 1956. Wayne Altree, Philip Bagby, Sir Ernest Barker, W. Boer, George Catlin, Christopher Dawson, Abba Eban, Edward Fiess, Pieter Geyl, Walter Kaufmann, Hans Kohn, H. Michell, Hans J. Morgenthau, Lewis Mumford, G. J. Renier, F. E. Robin, Pitirim Sorokin, O.H.K. Spate, Lawrence Stone, Kenneth W. Thompson, Iinus Walker, O.P., W. H. Walsh, Gotthold Weil.

Phyllis O'Callaghan, "A Selective Bibliography on A *Study of History*," *The Historical Bulletin*, Vol. XXXIV, pp. 161–181.

Rule-Crosby, *History and Theory*, Mouton & Co.: Netherlands, bibliography, Vol. IV, 2, pp. 212–233.

Pitirim A. Sorokin, *Modern Historical and Social Theories*, New York: Dover, 1963, pp. 113–120, 205–243.

CHAPTER NINE

THEOLOGY OF HISTORY AND THE

AUGUSTINIAN SPIRIT

It was noted that Augustine's thought constitutes what might properly be called a theology of history, concerned as it is with more than merely philosophically oriented history of the epistemological presuppositions of historical writing. The looseness of the term "philosophy of history" in current usage permits the inclusion of such figures as Augustine, Orosius, Joachim of Flora, and Bossuet in any general study of the philosophy of history, but it might be well to consider providential history more precisely for what it is, a theology of history, and consider it in its recent developments.[1]

As a theological science, a theology of history is preoccupied with the Providential plan of God in history and the degree to which such a plan is amenable to rational inquiry. Cultural his-

[1] The technical detailed exposition of a formal theology of history must be left to the theologians. As Karl Rahner has noted, this work has not been precisely outlined, but it usually concerns itself with basic themes, e.g., eschatology, the history of dogma, Providence, freedom, transcendence and immanence, the role of the Church. Such formal presentations would be Hans Urs von Balthasar, *A Theology of History* (New York: Sheed and Ward, 1963); J. V. Langmead Casserley, *Toward a Theology of History* (New York: Holt, 1965); Reinhold Niebuhr, *Faith and History* (New York: Charles Scribner's Sons, 1951); Oscar Cullmann, *Christ and Time* (Philadelphia: Westminster, 1964); Paul Tillich, *The Interpretation of History* (New York: Charles Scribner's Sons, 1936); Jean Daniélou, *The Lord of History* (Chicago: Regnery, 1958); and Henri-Irénée Marrou, *Theologie de l'histoire* (Paris: Vrin, 1968).

tory is studied in terms of the two factors of divine Providence and human freedom, and secular history itself is viewed in the light of the free response to the design of a beneficent God.

CONTEMPORARY THEOLOGIES OF HISTORY

A theology of history concerns itself in a special way with God's Revelation to his people. The idiom in such a revelation is often obscure, the scientific details inexact, but the great themes of God come through to his people.

To an Augustine there is a magnificent fulfillment of the Old Testament by the New. Professor James Harvey Robinson sees the Christian as perhaps the first to suspect the real grandeur of history. The divine epic begins at creation and looks ahead to the second coming when the definitive crisis between good and evil is to be resolved. History is not only open and adventuresome to the Christian, but as Harry Elmer Barnes observes, "Christian historiography was pragmatic to a degree not dreamed of by either Polybius or Dionysius." [2] Issues of salvation and damnation are at stake, and historically irreversible human decision acquires enormous importance.

Such theoretical importance of the historical event in the Christian tradition, however, would not be accepted by a Tatian or a Tertullian, who would see in such solicitude an inappropriate preoccupation with a passing world. Nor would it mean that a people given to allegorical interpretation of sacred texts would be sufficiently critical by modern standards to write good history, however important they might consider human choice.

The history of the theology of history as recorded in the works of Barnes, Thompson, and Shotwell, for example, reveals that the *Zeitgeist* of the period makes itself felt in this area as in all other realms. The Enlightenment, for instance, introduces a thought style inimical to supernatural values. Reason becomes

[2] Harry E. Barnes, A *History of Historical Writing* (New York: Dover, 1962), p. 43.

both divinity and its providence, and Voltaire becomes the prophet of the secular faith. The City of Man and its imminent and immanent problems replace preoccupation with transcendent and eternal destiny. Nietzsche's Zarathustra will proclaim "believe not those who speak of super-earthly hopes," and the philosopher himself will crusade against the Christian "nay saying" to life that drains away human energies from the only world that is real.

Within the Christian tradition itself, thought alternates from the incarnational to the transcendent—depending on the theologian's belief that the Christian should be involved in his world or hold himself and his chosen remnant aloof from its corruption.

To those who think of God as the "totally other" in a Barthian emphasis on transcendence, the metahistorical alone is principally significant; and man, the victim of his finiteness, finds his works as well as his nature comparatively feeble realities.

Incarnational thought usually concerns itself with an existentialist religious encounter of man with the person of Christ in a concrete historical situation, and is much more reflective of contemporary patterns of thought.

Rudolf Bultmann, for instance, declares that the essence of existence is "freedom from the past, openness for the future." [3] A future eschatology he conceives of as "apocalyptic myth." History achieves its significance, not alone in a distant *parousia*, but in the love that is brought to earthly encounters. Bultmann reflects on how the faith in a divine order and the security it engendered were shaken progressively by such forces as the Renaissance, the Reformation, the Enlightenment, the French Revolution, and Romanticism.

He sees Romanticism as particularly responsible for an historical relativism that would atomize knowledge and deny "a universal human reason which could conceive truths of timeless value." [4] Relativism creates for Bultmann a breakdown of belief

[3] Rudolf Bultmann, *Primitive Christianity in Its Contemporary Setting* (Cleveland, Ohio: World, 1966), p. 189.
[4] Rudolf Bultmann, *History and Eschatology* (New York: Charles Scribner's Sons, 1962), p. 9.

in an eternal teleological order and the absolute value of good-
ness or truth, as a result of which the "Christian Epic," as
Santayana called it, is fragmented into a series of historical inci-
dents ruled by economic laws. Man, the formerly autonomous
being, is seen at the mercy of historical conditions, and history
itself becomes sociology. Thus, for Bultmann the alternative to
a genuine *Heilsgeschichte* is a nihilism in which individuals and
events become meaningless episodes in a story which has no
unity or purpose.

It is to be noted that the theology of history is not in any
sense a recent discipline. From the Hebrew authors who set out
to write a theology of history to the Christian writers of today
who emphasize the eschatological dimension of God's relationship to his creation, the *Heilsplan* is a recognized pattern of
existence to a goal, although knowledge of intermediate situations is not claimed.

New Testament eschatology preserves the great themes of
providence, God's divine omnipotence as Lord of history, and
human freedom, but history is no longer open-ended. Fulfillment is found in Christ's incarnation, death, and resurrection.
The people of God, redeemed and made whole in Christ, await
the decisive moment of the Second Coming and its metahistorical end. The events of the intervening years are not only lived
in the aura of the Christian rebirth but, according to some theologians, in a "realized eschatology" in time.[5]

Henri de Lubac would be among those who would emphasize
the "realized" or incarnational in the Christian's involvement in
his world, feeling that traditional eschatology might engender a

---

[5] The term originates with the Anglican theologian, C. H. Dodd. Eschatology
traditionally has been a study of the "last things" and the great ultimate realities
of heaven, hell, death, and judgment. Bultmann sees it as developing from "the
concept of the periodicity of the course of worldly events" and specifically on
the periodicity of nature in the great-world-year. Cf. *History and Eschatology*,
p. 23; cf. also, David Tracy, *Eschatology: A Christian Approach to Time and
History* (Washington: Theological College, 1968), bibliography, pp. 348–351.
This privately printed volume, edited by Daniel F. Onley, is a collection of
Father Tracy's lectures assembled and edited by students.

farsightedness that would lure man from his world and its proper concerns.

John Macquarrie stresses the fact that Christian theology "takes its origin from a revelation given in a historical person rather than in a dateless myth or a timeless corpus of laws or of philosophical truths." [6] But considering speculative philosophies of history as suspect by the historical profession and no longer capable of eliciting interest, he too is interested primarily in the immediate problems of the significance of historical existence and the meaning of such statements that all human conditions are historically conditioned.

Hans Urs von Balthasar, in the first of the formal works on the subject previously referred to, centers his study on the pivotal fact of the Incarnation. Since Christ, all history is Christocentric, and the Christian judges all history from the point of view of a Christ who gives it ultimate meaning. It is the business of theology, the author maintains, to see how Christ stands in time and history as "the heart and norm" of the historical. [7]

Christ is seen as bringing a "final validity" to the historical process and effecting a seeming coalescence of world history and salvation history. Casserley phrases this relationship succinctly:

[6] John Macquarrie, *Principles of Christian Theology* (New York: Charles Scribner's Sons, 1966), p. 22. The author sees both the sense of history and the sense of eschatology as lost in the development of theology, and suggests that a rethinking of eschatology has been necessitated by two events: the collapse of "the classical scientific ideal in theology" and its Aristotelian vision of reality; and the progress made since Schweitzer in biblical renewal—a renewal in which eschatology is central. The methodology suggested is "horizon analysis," an evaluation made from an observer's determinate field of vision in the light of mutually conditioning subjective and objective factors. Man can expand his horizon through "a critical analysis of his own experience," and move on to new intellectual discovery. Karl Rahner says that eschatology affirms "the intrinsic finitude and historical nature of time; the uniqueness of the human act in relation to general eschatology; incarnation, death, and Resurrection; the "givenness" of an historical end; post-Christian temporality and Judgment; the beatific vision; the metaphysical nature of "glorified corporeality." It is important to note that in contemporary theology, the "last days" have already begun in Christ. Cf. Karl Rahner and Herbert Vorgrimler, *Theological Dictionary* (New York: Herder and Herder, 1965); and Karl Rahner, *Theological Investigations* (Baltimore: Helicon, 1966), I, pp. 211–212, IV, pp. 323–346.

[7] Hans Urs von Balthasar, *op. cit.*, pp. 19–20.

"The basic theme of human history is a religious theme, because that too is the basic theme of human history." [8] He considers "mere" secular history as comparatively meaningless, encapsulated as it is in mere temporality. Rejecting speculative philosophies of history as found in such writers as Vico, Hegel, Marx, and Spengler, and the possibility of formulating laws or prophesying the future, Casserley does see the possibility of arriving at some awareness of what history is all about.[9]

TEILHARD DE CHARDIN

Perhaps the most provocative of the theologies of history is not technically a theology at all; this is the theory of the great priest-paleontologist, Pierre Teilhard de Chardin (1881–1955).

If, as Teilhard once said, "Everything must pass through the crucible of thought," his concerns must be recognized to have a philosophical as well as a theological and paleontological dimension.

Teilhard asks the hard questions about the nature and destiny of man in the cosmic context of his world, and if he ventures on the terrain of the future, traditionally forbidden to the historian, it is because his scientific study of man's development in time and space has inevitable historical significance.

F. G. Elliott observes:

His philosophy is actually history. It is concerned not only with the world of our own day but with its past, not only with its present state, but with the unfolding of its entire existence. . . . It is a universe considered in its limitless space and in its remotest past with an eye always fixed on the point at which its future opens out into the infinite. No term could define Père Teilhard's philosophy more exactly nor provide a more precise point for comparison than

[8] J. V. Langmead Casserley, op. cit., pp. 69–70.
[9] Casserley considers philosophy of history to consist in the examination of historical methodology, an epistemological appraisal of the kinds and validity of historical knowledge, and most important "an ontological interpretation of the place and significance of historical events in what we may call the scale of being or reality." Ibid., p. 216.

the expression "Universal History," which, when used in Bossuet's sense, becomes an extension of Sacred History.[10]

Teilhard felt that apart from anthropocentric and anthropomorphic considerations, he could discern a well marked direction and progress of life that would be ultimately capable of empirical verification.[11] His is not so much the arrogantly assertive gnosticism of a Spengler as much as the sober speculation of the priest-scientist who sees the future in terms of consequence as well as prophecy. He sees reality in a total vision and history as the teleological development of a unified cosmic process in which man in his wholeness is a particularly meaningful part.

The search for wholeness prompts Chardin to go beyond the particularized views of the individual sciences to see the universe as a developing totality in which a universal will to live converges and is "hominized." [12]

Man as historian sees cosmic process both as experience and vicarious vision of the past. Like Ortega and Dilthey, Teilhard studies man in the conditioning context of his world. Like Hegel, he sees history as a progress in consciousness. Like Croce, he sees isolated matter as a meaningless residue when divorced from the total human experience. Cosmos for Teilhard is the developing starting point. Even elemental matter is impregnated with unity, plurality and energy, and the complex interweaving of forces of nature and person constituting the "science of the real" becomes history.

The Phenomenon of Man, particularly, has as its primary purpose the description of those inner purposive configurations behind the diverse elements in history. The universe presents a

[10] F. G. Elliott, "The World View of Teilhard de Chardin," International Philosophical Quarterly, I (December, 1961), pp. 643-644.

[11] Pierre Teilhard de Chardin, *The Phenomenon of Man (New York: Harper and Row, 1965), pp. 142, 146. This is a work of description and explanation of the evolutionary process in its successive stages: the pre-life (la prévie), the vital phase, the "thought phase," and the super life (la survie).

[12] Pierre Teilhard de Chardin, The Future of Man (New York: Harper and Row, 1964), pp. 11-36. Cf. also John V. Walsh, "History in the Phenomenon of Man," The World of Teilhard, Robert Francoeur (ed.) (Baltimore: Helicon, 1961), p. 131.

struggle between unorganized and unified multitudes. Energy is conceived as radial and tangential, the former a force that brings elements into greater complexity, the latter a unifying force of similarly structured elements. The historical development of the cosmos is charted by significant evolutionary "critical points," the first of which is the appearance of life.[13] Teilhard presents an arresting vision of the relationship of the world of man and the world of nature, seeing in the totality of nature the distention of a transcendent intelligence. The universe is an evolution, a growth process involving irreversible multiplication. From multiplication of cells comes organization which is teleologically progressive in character.

Not only is growth irreversible, but it goes through identical dialectical patterned phases of divergence, convergence, and emergence, which exhibit a gradualism of development, and an ordered progression from molecular to cellular life.

Teilhard has perhaps caught the imagination of the world precisely because he concerns himself with the fascinating, if unverifiable, possibilities of the future. He is not the only historian of the development of reality from cosmos to hominization, the progression to thought and reflection, but he also plays the seer's role in following evolutionary history into the realm of possibility, particularly in the area of consciousness. He sees the true evolution of the world taking place in the souls of men and in their mutual union, and asserts that its inmost agents are not mechanistic, but psychological and moral.

Evolution proceeds in the realm of the mind, and mind's distinctive product, civilization, is produced; urban civilization is its most sophisticated development. The continued thrust of consciousness through socialization and continued hominization leads to the ultimate point of convergence—what Teilhard calls Omega Point.[14]

[13] Life's progression itself is for Teilhard measurable. Brain complexity keeps pace with evolution until the "direct cerebralization" which points to man. With man the earth finds its soul.

[14] On the convergence of person and Omega Point, cf. Chapter Two, "The Phenomenon of Man" pp. 257–272.

Teilhard further suggests that the historical process must be conducted in freedom if mankind is successfully to evolve.[15] Ultimately, man finds his meaning in greater love and greater knowing in Omega Point. The growth of freedom, constituting as it does a growth in responsibility, allows for the possibility of error and evil. Man has the awesome power to decide human triumph and human failure.

Christian dogma itself culminates in union with God, the "Center of Centers." The Church is identified as "the portion of the world reflexively made Christ," the point of convergence between the cosmos and Omega Point.

These observations do not even constitute a summary of Teilhard's complex and detailed historical ideas, but they do indicate the dynamic and linearly progressive character of his thought.[16] Teilhard differs markedly from more statically conceived theological conceptions, but agrees with the basic Augustinian structure of free man working through irreversible history to his own "totalization" and ultimately to a transcendent goal. Man shares his creative talents with a divine Christ by whom history remains forever transfigured and in whom man grows in knowledge and love.[17]

MARITAIN

Jacques Maritain (1882–   ), the distinguished French scholar, overcoming an admitted prejudice against the very notion

[15] Teilhard discusses contemporary competing ideologies in *Building the Earth* (New York: Dimension Books, 1965). He laments both fascism and egalitarianism as political distortions.

[16] Cf. Teilhard's treatment of progress in *The Future of Man* (New York: Harper and Row, 1966), pp. 11–36, 61–81.

[17] *The Divine Milieu* (New York: Harper and Row, 1965), pp. 128–156. Cf. also Henri de Lubac, *Teilhard de Chardin, the Man and His Meaning* (New York: Mentor, 1965), p. v. "He to whom it is given to see Christ *more real* than any other reality in the World, Christ everywhere present and made great, Christ the final determination and plasmatic Principle of the Universe—that man lives in a zone where no multiplicity can distress him and which is nevertheless the most active workshop of universal fulfillment."

of a philosophy of history based on a distrust of Hegel, makes what he calls "a tentative approach" to the problem, and gives an added dimension to a basically Augustinian vision of history.[18]

He approaches the subject under four main divisions: the philosophy of history in general, the validity of axiomatic formulas or functional laws, the validity of typological formulas or vectorial laws, and God and the mystery of the world.

He identifies Augustine's *City of God* as the first great example of a philosophy of history, asserting that "Christianity has taught us that history has a direction, that it works in a determined direction. History is not an eternal return." [19] But he recognizes the theological dimension in man's attempt to see what he calls the "trans-historical" meaning of history, the meaning of the sequence of historical events.

Maritain does not consider history a science because of its preoccupation with the singular and contingent, although he recognizes that even the "raw" fact presupposes many critical and discriminating judgments and "analytical recastings."

Even if the object of philosophy of history is not scientific in the empirical sense, it can be a systematized body of wisdom, constituting as it does a content inducted from historical data. To Maritain, the philosophy of history is a branch of moral philosophy, utilizing the inductive light of facts and the rational light of philosophical analysis—the final application of philosophy to mankind moving through history.

History itself, for Maritain, is not a pretentious gnosticism, not a problem for which a solution is to be found, but a mystery to be contemplated. It is a mystery that involves the "supra-intelligible" purposes of God and the "infra-intelligible" activities of man, whose significance can only be partially understood. But history, he feels, "can be characterized, interpreted, or

[18] Charles Journet, in an article entitled "D'une philosophie chrétienne de l'histoire et de la culture," *Jacques Maritain, son oeuvre philosophique* (Paris: 1949), pp. 33–61, surprised Maritain by suggesting that he had made several divagations into the field of the philosophy of history. Maritain considers the Journet article "an indispensable complement" to his own work, *On the Philosophy of History* (New York: Charles Scribner's Sons, 1957).

[19] *Ibid.*, p. 2.

deciphered in a certain measure and as to certain general aspects —to the extent to which we succeed in perceiving in it meanings or intelligible directions, and laws which enlighten events without necessitating them." [20]

This intelligibility Maritain feels to be dependent upon the recognition of the free person and the existence of God—an approach he recognizes as alien to those who would see history as developing by a kind of inner necessity or scientific law, or by cyclic recurrence.

But more properly a theology of history must inevitably be a salvation history centered on the Kingdom of God and the mystery of the Church.

When Maritain talks of axiomatic formulas or functional laws, he refers to certain basic formulas or fundamental characteristics that history does seem to indicate. By vectorial laws he means the more detailed statements which deal with history's development in typical phases or directions.

Maritain's treatment of these laws, both true and false, is secondary to his main preoccupation in the philosophy of history with the crucial problem of the relation of divine and human freedom. He sees both the grandeur and the mystery of the *Heilsplan*, although he cautions against considering God's eternal plan as "a kind of scenario written in advance." [21]

Maritain, as a man of faith, is neither the optimistic naturalist, nor the dire pessimist, and he is concerned about avoiding what he calls the "theocratic illusion," the making of our world into the Kingdom of God.

DAWSON

Perhaps none of the new Augustinians has contemplated the mystery with greater skill than the English scholar, Christopher

---

[20] *Ibid.*, p. 33.
[21] Maritain's entire essay, "God and the Mystery of the World," *ibid.*, pp. 119–176, should be read to derive the full implications of his position.

Dawson (1889–   ), who considers any culture essentially a spiritual community "which owes its unity to common beliefs and a common attitude to life far more than to any uniformity of physical type." [22]

It is incidental to his work on world culture that Dawson considers world history in its theological implications, and it is a corollary to his belief in the natural character of man's religious instincts that he considers history as determined to a large degree by spiritual reality.[23]

Dawson is particularly significant among the new Augustinians, not because he is trying to suggest an empirical foundation for historical speculation, but because he sees the need for an interdisciplinary anthropological, sociological, and theological expertise in him who would try to understand the human experience.[24]

He is critical of both Spengler and Toynbee and suggests that history, more than a comparative study of the principal civilizations, must be a synoptic consideration of their constituent cultures; he is critical also of cyclic theory inasmuch as he believes that supercultures or world civilizations like Hellenism, Christianity, or Islam are theoretically capable of independent growth unless they are physically obliterated or absorbed by a larger culture.

A culture is formed and modified by race (the genetic factor), environment (the geographical factor), function (the economic factor), and thought (the psychological factor). Dawson judges such a culture primarily as the external manifestation of a spiritual life, and as a response to specific environmental conditions.

[22] Christopher Dawson, *The Age of the Gods* (New York: Sheed and Ward, 1934), p. 22. The best single work available on Dawson is *Dynamics of World History*, John J. Mulloy (ed.) (New York: Sheed and Ward, 1956). Cf. also Daniel A. O'Connor, *The Relation Between Religion and Culture According to Christopher Dawson* (Montreal: 1952).

[23] *Ibid.*, p. 23.

[24] Dawson sees history as concerned with the genetic growth or developmental aspects of human society, sociology as concerned with the structure of the same society. Systematic description and genetic analysis are thus complementary. Cf. Mulloy, *op. cit.*, p. 20.

Dawson observes at the conclusion of his work, *Progress and Religion:*

> We have followed the development of human culture through the ages, and have seen how at every step the religion of a society expresses its dominant attitude toward life and its ultimate conception of reality. Religion is the great dynamic force in social life, and the vital changes in civilization are always linked with changes in religious beliefs and ideals.[25]

As E. I. Watkin has observed, Dawson's work is a variation on the one central theme of the worship of a transcendent God as the essential constituent of a living culture, and that the progress of a culture is dependent on the vitality of the religion in question.[26]

It is in his early work, *Enquiries*, that Dawson considers in detail the problem of civilization cycles.[27] He sees the world divided into four great cultures—the European, Islamic, Indian, and Chinese. The common consciousness which gives unity to any culture is particularly reflected in religion, secondarily in philosophy and art. Dawson sees all cultures going through the process of growth, maturation, and possible decay. In the period of growth, a culture is still dominated by the synthesis of its predecessors; in the period of progress, the young culture becomes deciduous, as it were, and gradually sheds the older culture; the period of maturation is the period of coordination when there is an integration of the cultural forces.

Growth may be marked by crisis which is resolved either into synthesis or decay, as crisis cannot continue indefinitely.

But there are two rhythmic movements in the history of civilization which provide physical and psychical renewal respectively. There is never a period of complete arrest; "even while the outer

---

[25] * *Progress and Religion* (New York: Sheed and Ward, 1960, p. 185.
[26] This theme is particularly reflected in Dawson's Gifford lectures from 1947–1949: *Religion and Culture* (New York: Sheed and Ward, 1948); in *Religion and the Rise of Western Culture* (New York: Sheed and Ward, 1950); and in his earlier work, *Enquiries into Religion and Culture* (London: Sheed and Ward, 1933).
[27] *Enquiries*, pp. 67–94.

body of a civilization decays, its inner life is renewed, and by its transmission to a daughter culture becomes the fertilizing principle of a new age." [28]

Because of his background, especially in the areas of sociology and history, Dawson is opposed to the intellectualism of Hegel and the morphological apriorism of Spengler which tend to ignore both scientific and human individual contributions to the comprehension of history. And he does not wholly subscribe to Toynbee's thesis that cultures die from within, citing the destruction of Peruvian culture by the Spaniards, the destruction of the culture of the Danube provinces by barbarian invaders in the fifth century, and the Mongol destruction of the cities of eastern Iran.[29]

In his study, "Oswald Spengler and the Life of Civilizations," Dawson makes a strong case for the continuity of cultural trends through succeeding civilizations, although, as Mulloy puts it, "they must descend into the world of matter and time and suffer the hazards and misadventures to which human societies are subjected." [30]

Cultural integration and progress can be understood only by weighing both the spiritual and conditioning material elements. These factors would include not only divine providence, but the dynamism of a particular people and the natural character of a given region during a specific age. Both growth and stabilization are dependent upon the non-determined realization of creative potentialities.

The culture itself is studied not only under its most revealing aspects in religion, art, philosophy, science, and language, but in terms of its general commonly held value system which is unconsciously assumed or formally held.

Dawson recognizes the paradox that Christianity, while liberating man from a static cyclicism, never quite forgets that it

[28] *Ibid.*, p. 68.
[29] Cf. Mulloy, *op. cit.*, p. 437.
[30] *Ibid.*, p. 437.

stands as a challenge to the passing and temporal. But he feels that "Christianity has always possessed an organic relation to history which distinguishes it from the great Oriental religions and philosophies." [31] He goes on to say that Christianity can never really ignore history for the reason that it is an historical religion. For history is not "the sphere of completely rationalized human action," but a world in which the supra-rational and the infra-rational are also determinative. Good and evil will both find social expression in the historical experience. Christ is the fulfillment of historical purpose.

Dawson himself seemed to hint at a "realized" eschatology as early as 1939, when he said that to the Christian the world is always ending, because of his belief in the centrality of the Incarnation. The Church lives as the organ of the Spirit of God through history. Christian man lives as a free agent, but in a vital relationship to his God. His faith neither insulates him from crisis nor promises serenity in the midst of turmoil. The Christian simply rejects a completely secular view of the world and asserts (though he is unable to prove it to a naturalist's satisfaction) that faith is a meaningful encounter with the God of history.

Dawson employs the word "metahistory" to refer to a concern for the nature and meaning of history, and the cause and significance of historical change.[32] In this sense, metahistory is not only concerned with history's end, but with its vital temporal processes as unified by a spiritual principle.[33]

It might be said that Dawson, in considering a transcendent God the end of history, does not minimize historically conditioned temporal values.[34]

---

[31] *Ibid.*, p. 275. From the chapter "Christianity and Contradiction in History," pp. 262–286.

[32] Cf. "The Problem of Metahistory," Mulloy, *op. cit.*, pp. 287–293.

[33] Dawson, *The Modern Dilemma* (New York: Sheed and Ward, 1932), pp. 42–47, 94. Cf. also *Religion and the Modern State* (New York: Sheed and Ward, 1935), p. 134; and *Beyond Politics* (New York: Sheed and Ward, 1939), p. 82.

[34] *Religion and Culture* (New York: Sheed and Ward, 1948), pp. 208–209.

MARROU

Henri Marrou's work, *Théologie de l'histoire*, is particularly the fruit of his study of Augustine, and especially of that author's *City of God*. He sees it as crucial to the human experience to ascertain whether or not man is a child of God or merely a citizen of a temporal order. Every human being thus plays a role in a history other than that of the natural order; he has a spiritual history and participates as a free being in a *Heilsgeschichte* which looks to an end that is an eternal beginning.[35]

Marrou is also fascinated by the relationship of the theory of progress in Christian growth to maturity. As has already been observed, both secular progressivism and eschatological futurism exhibit a common linear structure, but in Christianity the term of history is also fulfillment.[36] Like Nietzsche, Marrou sees secular progress as a distorted derivation of Christian eschatology, and like Maritain he sees an ambivalence and mystery in history that man can only partially understand.

But he also sees man, hopefully working within the Providence of God, as capable of improving both self and world in the midst of adversity and evil.

"If one can identify the Christian vision of history as optimistic, it is a question of a tragic optimism which is assertive of faith and hope, despite the very difficult and very palpable reality of evil which we see in retrospect and in our daily experience." [37]

Marrou recognizes the ambivalence and the tragedy, but not the absurdity in the human situation. Echatological history is not an unbroken triumphal march from Paradise to *parousia*, but a twofold movement of progress and retrogression in which the wayfarer makes his way with often obscured vision through the *civitas terrena* to the *civitas Dei*.

Marrou sees human struggle and fulfillment particularly

[35] *Théologie de l'histoire*, p. 21.
[36] Cf. *Ibid.*, "Vrai et faux progrès," pp. 45–48.
[37] *Ibid.*, p. 50 (my translation).

through the Augustinian image of profane time, precarious, passing, and elusive, and time fulfilled into an eternal now. His vision of the two cities, like Rahner's vision of the natural and supernatural, does not have the cosmetic nicety of neatly divided realities. Man lives in a universe that is one, whose loves and attitudes are often inextricably intertwined, and whose Church exhibits less definable frontiers than in a former and less complicated day. But doubt and ambiguity need not produce paralysis; they may well produce a more becoming humility and compassion in which man resists the temptation to anticipate perfection in himself and in his institutions, and is satisfied to strive for his salvation in a flawed world. To recognize the flawed nature of the human enterprise is to recognize the flawed dimension of human institutions. Even a divinely instituted Church is not less a vehicle of divine purpose because it is a church of sinners, however much the insecure would seek in her a concretized immobility in the name of stability.[38]

Marrou appeals to Augustine's musical imagery to explain the apparent discord of history.[39] Augustine had identified the passing of time in the secular order as *tamquam pulcherrimum carmen*, an exquisite melody, in which theme and counter themes appear and disappear, and normal sound conveys meaningful subtleties. Marrou likens the unfolding of history to "an immense concert," although he does not point out in detail the severe limitations of the aesthetic product when only the conductor knows the entire score. The image itself can be carried through in the discordant elements of tragedy and schism Marrou sees in the contemporary world. Mankind is called by grace, but only a remnant will respond. It is the time of the Church in a special sense when a missionary summons to the people of God takes place, and a creative response is sought; and man must respond if he would realize the purpose of his existence.

[38] *Ibid.*, pp. 71–79.
[39] Toynbee centuries later is to talk of the harmony of the world ecumenical community in terms of an organ diapason. Cf. *Study of History*, Vol. VII, p. 734.

Karl Rahner has posed the precise relationship between individual and general salvation as one of the unresolved questions
of eschatology. The historian of providence can indeed accept
the fact of universality of providence and his own freedom, but
the old question remains: granted that God wills it, what is it
that God wills?

Daniélou has observed that a theology of history became possible only when Christianity became aware of the fact of its own
duration. He would, of course, agree that the Hebrews too were
particularly aware of a destiny, however limited the manner in
which their destiny was spelled out.

A final point in the theology of history concerns the future.
As has been observed, the future plays a greater role in eschatological thought than in the thought of the critical historian for
whom the future is a forbidden terrain. But religious hope is
usually oriented to the future, and Daniélou particularly, sees
a "special connexion between hope and history." [40] Its object
he sees as the final destiny of the world and of the whole human
race as opposed to a concern for the individual.

The theology of history thus would seem to be concerned in
a special way with duration, the historical dimension, not because time is the essential content, but perhaps because it is the
most revealing characteristic by which history's fulfillment may
be at least partially understood.

SUGGESTED READINGS

Hans Urs von Balthasar, A *Theology of History*, New York: Sheed and
    Ward, 1963, pp. 47–76.
Rudolf Bultmann, *History and Eschatology*, New York: Harper and Row,
    1962, pp. 23–73; *Primitive Christianity In Its Contemporary Setting*,
    New York: Meridian, 1956, pp. 180–182.
Herbert Butterfield, *Christianity and History*, New York: Charles Scrib-
    ner's Sons, 1950, pp. 93–146.

[40] *The Lord of History*, p. 353.

J. V. Langmead Casserley, *Toward A Theology of History*, New York: Holt, 1965, pp. 188–215.

Oscar Cullmann, *Christ and Time*, Philadelphia: Westminster Press, 1962. For primitive Christianity's conception of time and history, this whole volume should be read.

Jean Daniélou, *The Lord of History*, Chicago: Regnery, 1958, Ch. VIII: "Notions of Eschatology," pp. 269–278. Perhaps the clearest short presentation of this subject.

Dynamics of World History (Christopher Dawson) John J. Mulloy (ed.), New York: New American Library, 1956: "Christianity and the Meaning of History," pp. 233–286.

Karl Jaspers, *The Origin and Goal of History*, New Haven: Yale University Press, 1956, pp. 213–230.

Jacques Maritain, *On The Philosophy of History*, New York: Charles Scribner's Sons, 1957, Ch. IV: "God and the Mystery of the World," pp. 119–163.

Henri-Irénée Marrou, *Théologie de l'histoire*, Paris: 1968, pp. 21–94.

Reinhold Niebuhr, *Faith and History*, New York: Charles Scribner's Sons, 1951, pp. 214–244.

CHAPTER TEN

PHILOSOPHY OF HISTORY AND THE

CULTURAL MOOD

It has been suggested that man's vision of historical reality is ultimately reducible to progressivism—religious or secular— and cyclic recurrence, and that any other outlook represents variations on these two basic themes. It is quite possible, however, to view the historical experience as dysteleology; i.e., a fragmented movement toward no purposeful end, but toward a future determined only by the limitations of human potential and the external situation that represents an earlier historical articulation of that potential. The progressive secularization of European thought from Augustine's time did not affect the basic linear way of viewing history, but it did to a large degree substitute as a political goal an antiseptic Babylon for the heavenly Jerusalem. Secularism retained the form while altering the substance of the historical experience. Modern man tended to reject eschatological linearism as well as cyclicism in favor of a secular futurism, linear in structure and destined to a purely earthly goal. But contemporary man is a more cautious species who is no longer deluded by the inevitability of progress or the perfectibility of man. He is inclined to devote his attention to his immediate psychological and environmental concerns, a preoccupation that is particularly reflected in the philosophy of existentialism.

Existentialist thought varies widely from the God-intoxicated thought of Kierkegaard to the atheistic naturalism of Nietzsche, but as Paul Tillich has said, existentialism has become the style of our period in all areas of life.

> . . . Existentialism in the Western intellectual world starts with Pascal in the 17th century, has an underground history in the 18th century, a revolutionary history in the 19th century, and an astonishing victory in the 20th century.[1]

It might also be said that the existentialist attitude is not necessarily sympathetic to the genetic attitude of historical interpretation found in the "new" history of Teggart and Robinson. In the emphasis on the present, the existentialist implies that a "new" history rooted in the past is already old.

In the existentialist mood, impatient with orthodoxies, scientism, progress, systems, and what is felt to be rationalistic oversimplification of reality, man tends to evaluate his experience less as a rationally derived and charted voyage to a meaningful end and more as a series of encounters between man and the existent "now" of his world; less a preoccupation with the sanctified or unlamented past, or the direction of a luminous or forbidding future, than with the possibilities of the moment in an actually existent world that exhibits no bias in favor of order and fulfillment. Existentialism is also a protest against the depersonalizing elements of a mechanism that evaluates man in terms of objective function, although it recognizes the ambiguity and anguished isolation of human life. Karl Jaspers (1883–1969) gave the name of *Grenzsituationen*, limit or border situations, to the ultimate situational experiences of anxiety, guilt, despair, and sense of threatened finitude with which the existential philosophical quest begins. Man organizes his search for a transcendent unifying Other in the idiom of metaphysics, but his life is lived in the empirical world in which he must find such peace as is to be found.

Ortega y Gasset (1883–1955), Spain's most articulate modern

---

[1] "Existentialism and Psychotherapy" in *Psychoanalysis and Existential Philosophy*, H. M. Ruitenbeck (ed.) (New York: Dutton, 1962), p. 5.

philosopher, expresses the intimacy of this creative tension between man and his environment in his famous phrase "I am I
and my circumstance".[2] The subject and his world are inseparable, and one cannot be understood without the other. He goes
on to say that not only is man himself and his circumstance,
but if he does not "save" his circumstance, he does not save
himself.[3] Circumstance for Ortega means everything except
the ego—but the everything with which the ego is constantly
involved. "To live is to deal with the world, to direct oneself
to it, to act in it, to busy oneself in it." [4]

Jean Paul Sartre (1905–   ) regards man as a self-enclosed
absurdity, a useless passion whose meaning is found (if at all),
not in a providentially ordered history, but in more or less frustrated responses to his environment and the challenges it presents. Man can ask questions of his world and freely act on the
answers his world seems to yield; he can arrive at a kind of self
knowledge. But phenomenological description is the closest man
can get to ontological ultimacy.

There are no ultimate realities or values which can be norma-
tive, but there is an historical framework in reality that is equivalent to its succeeding manifestations. Sartre accuses Nietzsche
of attempting to restore the Absolute in the guise of a law of
cyclic return—as if to suggest the human psychological need for
some ultimate ground of isolated historical experiences. Sartre

[2] Ortega's humanistic concern for the individual in his environment, creating
his world, is reminiscent of Dilthey and Vico. Life is a task that man freely
undertakes. The substitution of "vital reason" for the abstract "pure reason" is
literally what Ortega feels to be the mood of our time—as expressed in his work
El tema de nuestro tiempo (Obras, Madrid: 1932, III, pp. 141–203—translated
as The Modern Theme, New York: Peter Smith, 1933). Cf. Christian Ceplecha,
The Historical Thought of Jose Ortega y Gasset (Washington: 1958).

[3] ". . . Y si no la salvo a ella, no me salvo yo." Obras, I, p. 322.

[4] Ibid., II, p. 607. The present mood, as has been suggested, has little to do
with progress in its traditional optimistic sense. It is Kierkegaardian and Pascalian
anguish that has done more to create the contemporary mood than the roseate
expectations of the progressivists who dominated European thought for more
than a century. But the turn of the century saw the weakening of progressivist
theory. The neat and orderly Newtonian universe and social optimism both col-
lapsed under the impact of more sophisticated scientific theory and the advent
of an era that was to bring two devastating world wars.

himself, of course, assumes the nonexistence of a Lord of History in what Collins has called a "postulatory atheism," i.e., a God-denying attitude assumed without a detailed analysis of the content and techniques of theistic philosophers.[5]

Sartre's hero, Roquentin, for instance, in Nausea, sees the phenomena of the world reducible to no meaningful pattern, but as independent thrusts into an enigmatic existence which brings neither joy nor redemption. "I was Roquentin," says Sartre. "I used him to show, without complacency, the texture of my life." [6]

And the good pagan, Albert Camus (1913–1960), presents the classic portrayal of rootless, alienated, existential man in the character of Meursault in The Stranger, doomed in the manner of all of Camus' heroes to agonizing isolation and eventual destruction.[7] To Camus, as to Kafka, man is victim, but he can bring raw courage and nobility even to the battle he cannot win. Camus too sees man in "that magnificent yet futile matter which we call the present," rather than in the past or future. This is probably to be attributed to his early philosophic interest in Pascal and Kierkegaard, as well as to the influence of his teacher, Jean Grenier, a philosophical essayist primarily concerned with specific problems of existence rather than with abstract theorizing.

There is a nobility in Camus, who sees himself too destitute of wisdom or virtue to transform his world or mankind, but nonetheless sees his role "to serve in my place, those few values without which a world, even transformed, isn't worth living . . ." [8] He sees misfortunes themselves possessed of a "solar

[5] Cf. James Collins, *The Existentialists (Chicago: Henry Regnery, 1952), pp. 38–79; cf. also David E. Roberts, *Existentialism and Religious Belief (New York: Oxford University Press, 1959), pp. 193–226.

[6] The Words, the Autobiography of Jean Paul Sartre (New York: Random House, 1964), p. 251.

[7] "Everything ends by no one listening," as the old man says in L'Envers et l'endroit. Other frustrated heroes in Camus are Jan in Le Malentendu, Nancy in his adaptation of Faulkner's Requiem for a Nun, Kaliayev in Les Justes, Diego in L'Etat de Siège.

[8] Cf. Germaine Brée's brilliant study, *Camus (New York: Columbia University Press, 1964).

brilliancy that engender their own consolation," and life itself made bearable by moments of beauty and lucidity.

His is not so much a formal argumentation against the possibility of God, as a new atheism which consists in the affirmation of exclusively human values and the recognition of what is felt to be the fact of the cultural rejection of God. It might be added that Camus rejected any theory that claimed for historical events a meaningful orientation, Marxian or otherwise; and it goes without saying that he rejected any philosophic or religious apriorism which would prejudge the case of man as he actually exists. A further characteristic of Existentialism is its elitism, implied in Sartre and Camus, and developed in depth by Ortega in his *Revolution of the Masses*.

The phenomenological tradition of Edmund Husserl (1859–1938) and Martin Heidegger (1889–   ) emphasizes the reality of things themselves. Heidegger, particularly, represents the fusing of existential and ontological concern, and his influence on Sartre is particularly marked. Husserl's philosophical aim was to take a fresh look at reality through immediate intuition—a position suggestive of Camus' observation that to think is to learn how to see anew—and to describe it in its existential objectivity without benefit of preconceptions, systems, or diverting abstractions. In Husserl at least, this scrutiny was directed at the phenomenon of consciousness itself, not as ideally divorced from the extramental world, but consciousness as "intending" an object beyond itself. Heidegger's dislike of the emphasis on subjective consciousness impels him to concentrate his attention on being-in-the-world, that is, man concerned, not as an independent intelligence reacting to the world, but man as thrown into and structured in the world, subject to its pressures, free to choose his paths in the world, and whose successive experiences will constitute his history.

The theater of the absurd, too, is a particularly significant example of the dilemma of existential man. The works of Beckett, Ionesco, Duerrenmatt, Pinter, Genêt, Osborne, and Albee are among those which reflect concern for what critic Walter Kerr wearily calls the themes of the vending machine of truth in our time: the world is a jungle; no man knows who he is; each man wears a mask; we are all guilty.[9] Beckett shows the isolation of man by imprisoning him in jars and ashcans; Ionescu highlights depersonalization by seeing man as an animal (*Rhinoceros*); Genêt uses a maze of mirrors to expose man's terrifying solitude and his pointless efforts to evade relentless death.

Alienated man is also graphically presented by such writers as Updike, Salinger, Purdy, Arthur Miller, Baldwin, Mailer, and Ciofran.[10]

It is quite understandable that in the light of the contemporary existentialist-phenomenological mood, the so-called speculative philosophies of history, concerned with universal plans or patterns in the grand manner of Spengler and Toynbee, are diminishing in popularity. For historical consciousness inevitably looks over the shoulder of contemporary man like a distracted conversationalist, both to see what and where contemporary man has been. Neither the existentialist nor the phenomenologist is greatly interested in the past for its own sake. Theirs is a personalistic preoccupation with man in his present world, and neither archaism nor futurism is considered as either a relevant determinant or an inevitable consequence of the present. Old orthodoxies, systems, and universal generalizing no longer retain their power to elicit the support they received in an earlier era.

The analytic tradition, however, which represents the other significant trend in the world of philosophy—especially in England for more than a decade—is more concerned with the problem of the critical philosophy of history, i.e., the nature of historical knowledge, its epistemological presuppositions, and the validity of historical utterance. If the task of philosophy is not to think or talk of the world at all, but merely to analyze

---

[9] Cf. Martin Esslin, *The Theater of the Absurd* (New York: Doubleday, 1961).

[10] Cf. Sidney Finkelstein, *Existentialism and Alienation in American Literature* (New York: International Publishers, 1967).

the manner in which the world is thought and talked of, then what emerges from the analytic approach to history is a "descriptive metaphysic" which recognizes and evaluates the historical modality of both thought and utterance.[11] The philosophic task is a "therapy," as Wittgenstein was to call it, by which erroneous conceptions were to be reinvestigated by an examination of linguistic forms, not because the analyst is inordinately preoccupied with mere words, but because he believes that thought becomes amenable to scientific evaluation only to the degree to which it is capable of being expressed.[12]

The contemporary mood appears in sharp contrast to the Romantic spirit which gave great impetus to interpretative history. Both of these contemporary approaches are opposed to a classic rationalism, as is to be observed in the existentialist protests of Pascal and Kierkegaard against Cartesianism and Hegelianism respectively, and against the efforts of someone like G. E. Moore to arrive at knowledge of some truth, "however unimportant," merely because it is truth.

To understand the history written in an era is obviously to understand the age that produces it. The Romantic spirit produced interpretative history, as positivism, with its emphasis on the dimensive and sensibly verifiable, produced "factual" history which atomized experience into its verifiable components.

The age of classicism was an age of Reason, although the literary critic would at times limit classicism to problems of

[11] Arthur C. Danto, *Analytical Philosophy of History* (London: Cambridge University Press, 1965), p. vii. Professor Danto, who has been the first to construct such a "descriptive metaphysic of historical existence," observes that communication itself would be marginal in a people who thought "unhistorically." Cf. also Morton White, *Religion, Politics, and the Higher Learning* (Cambridge, Massachusetts: Harvard University Press, 1959): "A Plea for an Analytic Philosophy of History."

[12] M. J. Charlesworth suggests that the name "analysis" is as necessarily vague as "existentialism." Moore, Russell, Wittgenstein, Ayer, Wisdom, and Ryle, for instance, do not represent a common philosophy as much as a common thought-style in their general approach to philosophic problems. Analysts are not professionally interested in worldviews or global outlooks as much as with the relatively modest problems of linguistic accuracy and problems of clarification. Cf. *Philosophy and Linguistic Analysis* (Pittsburgh: Duquesne University Press, 1961), p. 3.

form rather than of content. Romanticism represented to some degree an abandonment of reason for feeling, imagination, and subjectivity. In literature, it represented a new emphasis on the creative poetic imagination; in religion, it represented a trend to a religion of feeling and emotion over what was felt to be a desiccated formalism based on duty and order. In history the Romantic spirit took the form of more imaginative theories of cultural evolution, aided by the rise of Darwinism and the inevitable extrapolations of organic imagery into the realms of social organization and historical explanation.[13]

It is important to remember that the philosophy of history was not a creation of romanticism, as its roots were to be found earlier in the seventeenth-century development of the philosophy of progress. But romanticism certainly did create a climate in which the interpretative philosophers could function and develop. The controversial writings of the Reformation and the synthesizing that was so much a part of the rationalist tradition had created a historical consciousness that would prove enormously helpful to later scholarship.

Romanticism was not concerned merely with biologism, for Spencer's consequent attempt to apply evolutionism to all human institutions was more reflective of a naturalistic positivism than the romantic tradition. Spencer's *Synthetic Philosophy*, though it was to become an obsolete synthesis, was really an astonishing rationalistic attempt to assemble social, psychological, and biological thought into one patterned context.

Nor does it seem correct to associate the romantic spirit too uncritically with the impassioned individualism of a Rousseau or the lyricism of a Goethe. For human freedom was to become less a reality in the new biologism; and scientific inquiry (never geared to the personal and subjective) was to address itself increasingly in the nineteenth century to discovering the latent mechanism of individual and collective behavior.

[13] Cf. for instance, Richard Hofstadter, *Social Darwinism in American Thought* (Boston: Beacon, 1962); and Harry Elmer Barnes, *An Intellectual and Cultural History of the Western World* (New York: Dover, 1965): "Intellectual Implications of the Theory of Evolution," pp. 956–964.

Romanticism was a human mood, and as a human mood it was the mood of the historian who was increasingly fascinated at the turn of the century with the irrational, the mysterious, and the undefinable in human behavior. The paradox consisted not only in the fact that it co-existed with a rationalistic philosophy of progress, but in the fact that the very romanticism which motivated the new vision of man, his society, and his history resulted often in an attempt to reduce these very elements to rational and even mechanistic dimensions, as exemplified in the psychological and social "engineering" of Freud and Durkheim.[14]

The romantic spirit also lent itself to a preference for gnostic insight—the brilliant *aperçu*—over sober analysis. Thus Spengler's attempted description of culture based on the principles of plant morphology was likened by the more sober of the academic community to the grievous probing of a deep and secret wound by a clumsy hand.

Perhaps the most significant contribution of the Romantic movement to historical writing was the crystallization of the mood in the movement of historicism. This was essentially a nineteenth century attempt, relativistic in inspiration, to go beyond flat assertion and conventional explanation by attempting to find the vital richness of the past in supposedly "nonhistorical" materials—language, legend, folk-song, law, customs, and the arts.[15]

Meinecke, the great German historian of the movement, suggests that the past can be truly understood only when one goes

[14] Sabine quotes Léon Brunschvicg as calling the search for a law of the growth and development of societies the "darling vice" of social thought in the nineteenth century.

[15] Cf. *The Varieties of History*, Fritz Stern (ed.) (New York: Meridian, 1959): "Historicism and Its Problems," by Friedrich Meinecke, pp. 267–288. Meinecke sees three modes of causality: the mechanistic, the biological, and the spiritual-moral, as three seals inextricably stamped on the face of history. ". . . Beyond the contingent operation of mechanistic causality the spontaneous acts of men may . . . intervene to interpret, divert, intensify, or weaken the morphology of events and so impart to history that complexity and singularity which makes a mockery of all attempts to explain it by invariable laws." *Ibid.*, p. 269. This classic historical essay should be read in its entirety. To Popper and D'Arcy, historicism is the search for laws or patterns of history which permit prophecy. Cf. Popper's *The Open Society and Its Enemies*, 1, p. 3; and D'Arcy's *The Meaning and Matter of History*, p. 10.

beyond the scientific and the merely causal to a sympathetic grasp of the past through "unmediated seeing," goes beyond the tiny perceived segment of the past called the "essential" to see the historical significance of those values beyond soil, sun, hunger, and love. He quite legitimately objects that to ignore a universe of minutiae and subjective tendencies out of a supposed solicitude for scientific objectivity is not only undesirable but impossible. The historian must always be concerned with a "living interest in the concrete content of material," and this interest may yield more than the great categories of obvious value. But there will also be a "supreme inclusive value" that will permit the integration of ideas and facts without the extremes of "ossified academicism" or "subjectivism run riot."

Quite obviously, the introduction of organic imagery into the historical vocabulary had great descriptive advantages, especially in the new emphasis on the developmental character of social institutions. Like the existentialists who were to come after them, the romanticists were deeply conscious of the inadequacy of classical rational inquiry, and often tended to mysticism and the subtler aspects of ideology.

It would, of course, be quite convenient in the history of thought of the last three centuries to see the streams as unpolluted by foreign elements. But as Sorokin has brought out in his discussion of socio-cultural systems, a dominant thought-style or *Zeitgeist* does not preclude the possibility of the simultaneous presence of different ideas.

To recognize a particular cultural mood is not to deny that certain basic questions will continue to be asked by men who are not interested merely in isolated narratives. The philosophy of history is a "natural" science in the sense that man cannot resist the temptation to ask how the isolated narratives hang together. It is also true that we live at an exciting hour when the horizons of knowledge have been enormously expanded and we have developed methodological tools which will prompt a secretive past to yield more of her secrets. It may indeed be impossible to provide definitive answers for even the most natural of questions, but the fact that the philosopher and the historian are not prophets need not deter them from trying to perceive some overall meaning to the process, and trying to express this meaning in the cultural idiom of their time.

Suggested Readings

Reynold Borzaga, *Contemporary Philosophy*, Milwaukee: The Bruce Publishing Company, 1966.
Germaine Brée, *Camus*, New York: Harcourt, Brace & World, Inc., 1964.
Maxwell John Charlesworth, *Philosophy and Linguistic Analysis*, Pittsburgh: Duquesne University Press, 1961.
Harvey Cox, *The Secular City*, New York: The Macmillan Company, 1965.
Leslie Dewart, *The Future of Belief*, New York: Herder and Herder, 1966.
Martin Esslin, *The Theatre of the Absurd*, Garden City, New York: Doubleday & Company, Inc., 1961. Analyses of the works of Beckett, Ionesco, Adamov, Genêt, Albee, Arrabal, Grass, Pinter, Simpson.
Sidney Finkelstein, *Existentialism and Alienation in American Literature*, New York: International Publishers, 1965.
Russell Kirk, *The Conservative Mind*, Chicago: Henry Regnery Company, 1960. A good introduction to the contemporary conservative tradition.
Remy C. Kwant, *The Phenomenological Philosophy of Merleau-Ponty*, Pittsburgh: Duquesne University Press, 1963.
G. Pitcher, *The Philosophy of Wittgenstein*, Englewood Cliffs, New Jersey: Prentice-Hall, 1964.
William J. Richardson, *Heidegger: Through Phenomenology to Thought*, The Hague: Nijhoff, 1963.
David Roberts, *Existentialism and Religious Belief*, New York: Oxford Galaxy Edition, 1959.
John K. Ryan, ed., *Twentieth Century Thinkers*, Staten Island, New York: Alba House, 1964. Brief studies of Bergson, Blondel, Gilson, Maritain, Marcel, Berdyaev, Toynbee, Husserl, Heidegger, Wittgenstein, Dewey, Freud, Jung, Unamuno, Sartre, Merleau-Ponty, and Tillich.
Arthur Schlesinger, Jr., *The Vital Center*, Cambridge, Massachusetts: The Riverside Press, 1962. A good introduction to the contemporary liberal tradition.
Paul Tillich, "The Conception of Man in Existential Philosophy," *Journal of Religion*, 19 (1939), p. 211.

EPILOGUE

The philosophy of history is not only a significant chapter in the history of ideas, but it is particularly reflective of the contemporary crisis of a generation which seeks increasingly to understand itself and the long-term significance of the events of our time. Not because all history, as Croce says, is contemporary history, but because every voyage into the past begins in a present whose concerns influence both inquiry and inquirer. Technology particularly has dramatized the modern dilemma in illuminating the past and the present, and the possibilities of the future. It has also revealed what Bertrand Russell has called its "ethical neutrality," and reminds us that science can heal and destroy with awesome brilliance, but that it cannot tell us which of the two we ought to do.

The development of the disciplines of psychology, economics, and sociology, the continued evaluation of our political and social institutions in the light of civic unrest and military involvements—these too are conducive to the synoptic view so intriguing to the philosopher of history.

The personalities and movements considered in this book represent the ultimate attitudes that man can assume in the presence of his history. When crisis assumes the proportions of the possible destruction of civilization as we know it, man can be lured away more easily from those parochial concerns which, in a calmer time, perhaps disproportionately consume his interest. In stress, he tends to ask more seriously if his experience adds up to something progressively meaningful, something meaningless, or something uniform that has basically the same meaning as it recurs in succeeding ages.

In a developing academic discipline, the philosopher of history has attempted to frame in a disciplined way what man, in his more reflective moments, thinks about his historical existence. He is not only the man who seeks the larger vision, but the man who appraises the objectivity and scientific character of the epistemological presupposition, evaluates the clarity of historical expression, and examines the validity of historical prophecy. He is often looked at askance by both critical historian and the professional philosopher because he does sometimes make divagations in more conventional areas of inquiry. But it seems in our time both appropriate and necessary to ask the questions that he asks even when the answers found are neither definitive nor wholly convincing. It is in this modest hope that this short volume has been prepared.

INDEX

Absolute Spirit, 111 ; in Hegel, 112f, 114f
Ages, in Vico, 60f
Albright, W. F., on Spengler, 98
Alienation, as contemporary mood, 166f
Anaximander, theory of the Boundless, 23
Anaximenes, cycle theory of, 23
Aristotle, and cyclicism, 27f
Aron, R., on philosophy of history, 9
Atheism, the "new," 166 ; in Nietzsche, 91
Augustine, St., as apologist, 34 ; The City of God, 47f ; dependence on a Jewish historical tradition, 39 ; on the epic of the two cities, 47f ; and human happiness, 36 ; on individual responsibility, 36 ; and linear history, 34–50 ; and the nature of history, 12 ; and Plato, 45 ; and recurrence theory, 35 ; and the Roman Empire, 46 ; on the sack of Rome, 45f ; and the theory of history, 143ff ; on uniqueness of the event in history, 37
Aurelius, M., modifies Stoic determinism, 29
Ayer, A. J., influence on Danto, 10

Balthasar, H., and the theology of history, 147
Barbarism, in Berdyaev, 61
Barnes, H. E., 3
Becker, C., 5 ; on historical fact, 7
Berdyaev, N., on the theory of progress, 15, 85
Berlin, I., 3
Bernheim, E., 6
Bodin, J., and the theory of progress, 70
Bossuet, J., and providential history, 12
Brandenbury, E., on Spengler, 98
Bultmann, R., and the theology of history, 145f
Burckhardt, J., 1
Bury, J. B., on progress, 85 ; on providential history, 12f

Cairns, G., on cyclical theory, 23
Camus, A., atheism in, 166 ; influence of Pascal and Kierkegaard on, 165 ; meaning in the thought of, 165f
Case, S. J., on the philosophy of history, 9
Casserly, J. V. L., on the theology of history, 148
Change, in Nietzsche, 92
Christianity, and imperial culture, 46f
Chronology, of Julius Africanus, 38
Chryssipus, and Stoic cyclicism, 28
Civilizations, breakdown of in Toynbee, 136f ; nature and growth of in Toynbee, 135f
Class struggle, in Marx, 80
Clement of Rome, on the nature of history, 37
Cochrane, C. N., on Augustine, 36
Cohen, M., 2 ; on Hegel, 119
Collingwood, R. G., on "apocalyptic" events, 13 ; critique of Spengler, 100 ; on Croce, 128 ; on history, 3 ; on the universality of Christian history, 12
Commager, H. S., 4, 6
Comte, A., and the birth of sociology, 76f ; and the function of sociology, 78 ; influence of, 78f, 79 ; and the Law of the Three Stages, 77f ; and the theory of progress, 75–79
Condorcet, M., and the theory of progress, 72ff
Cortés, J. D., 8
Cosmic Year, in classical thought, 25
Cosmogony, nature of Homeric, 31
Creationism, as nonclassical, 29 ; unknown in ancient world, 11
Critique, of Marx, 84f ; of the theory of progress, 84f
Croce, B., 8 ; anti-Hegelianism in, 129 ; the concept of "human" history in, 130 ; critique of historical causation, 129f ;

critique of philosophy of history, 129f; critique of pseudohistory, 131; and the facts of history, 131; and "meaning in history," 130; on the natural sciences and history, 128f; on the nature of history, 127–131; on philosophy as history, 7; "rethinking" of the past in, 129f; subjectivism in, 128f; on Vico, 63f

Cullman, O., on the remnant of Israel, 43

Culture, Faustian in Spengler, 102; ideational, idealistic, and sensate in Sorokin, 106; nature of in Dawson, 154ff

Cunning of Reason, in Hegel, 116

Cyclicism, 11; classical, 19–32; in Dawson, 155f; in Hinduism and Buddhism, 32; in Mesopotamia and Egypt, 31; origin of, 23; rigid Stoic form of, 28; and social institutions, 28

Danilevsky, N., critique of periodization, 95; laws of history in, 96f; theory of history in, 94–97

Danto, A. C., analytic philosophy of history of, 10

D'Arcy, M., on Vico, 59

Dawson, C., 2, 8; on Christianity, 156f; on civilization cycles, 155ff; on cultural continuity, 156; on Jewish tradition, 46; on the meaning of history, 153–158; on the nature of culture, 154ff; on theology of history, 12; on Toynbee, 134

Death of God theory, and Hegel, 115

Democritus, 29

Destiny, in Spengler, 100

Determinism, in Marx, 81

Development, in Teilhard de Chardin, 150f

Dilthey, W., 119–127; and empirical sciences, 120; freedom of man in, 120; and the historian's task, 126; and historical subjectivity, 126f; and human studies (Geisteswissenschaften), 122f; and the idealist tradition, 122f; and the influence of mathematical sciences, 120; influences on, 123; and intellectual history, 124; and intellectual systems, 121; and intuition as methodology, 123; and Kant, 124; on metaphysics, 122, 126f; on methodology, 123; pantheism in, 125; and the past, 126; and the philosophy of history, 120–127; and psychology, 124; on psychology and historical knowledge, 121f; on rationalist synthesis, 122; and the state, 127; vitalism in, 125

Disintegration, of culture in Toynbee, 137

Dray, W. H., 6; on philosophy of history, 10

Dualism, in Hegel, 112

Dysteleology, in history, 162

Edelstein, L., challenge to classical conception of progress of, 22

Eliade, M., on classical time, 29; on the sacred and profane, 30; on sacred time, 21

Epictetus, modifies Stoic determinism, 29

Epicureans, and cyclicism, 29

Eschatology, 146f; in Dawson, 157; and providential history, 16

Etherealization, in Toynbee, 136

Eusebius, and recurrence theory, 38

Evolutionism, in Teilhard de Chardin, 150

Existentialism, and history, 163f

Facts, and history, 7

Feuerbach, L., on God as an anthropological projection, 83; influence of on Marx, 80

Fontenelle, B., on progress, 69

Freedom, in Hegel, 116; in Marx, 81

Frisch, M., on recurrence, 20

Futurism, secular, 16

Gardiner, P., 6

Gibbon, E., as interpretative historian, 8

Goal of history, in Hegel, 114

God, in Hegel, 115; in Jewish history, 40

Godwin, W., and the theory of progress, 73

Goethe, J., on progress, 69

Gooch, G. P., on Dilthey, 123

Gnosticism, in the Romantic movement, 170

Greeks, and freedom, 19; and history, 20

Hegel, G., Absolute Spirit in, 112f, 114f; concept of freedom in, 116; concept of God in, 115; concept of individual in, 116f; concept of leader in, 117; on consciousness in history, 113; cunning of Reason in, 116; and death of God theory, 115; goal of history in, 114; the Idea in, 118; idea of history in, 112; idealistic monism in, 115; idiosyncrasy of Spirit in, 118; importance of, 119; on the individual in the state, 113f; and Kierkegaard, 116; on kinds of history, 111; and Marx, 83; on objectivization of God, 115; role of philosophy in, 119; the State in, 113f; theory of history in, 109–119; transcendence in, 115

Heraclitus, and change, 23

Herder, J. G., 9

Hero, in Greek tragedy, 20
Herodotus, 3
Hesiod, and cyclicism, 25; and the origin of cyclicism, 23
History, an antivital force in Nietzsche, 93; as art and science, 3f; as art and science in Croce, 127f; Augustinian, 12; classical patterns of, 10; compared with chronicle in Croce, 130f; definition of in Hegel, 112; definitive, 4; and discernible patterns, 14; and fact, 7; and fate, 19; and free will in Bodin, 70; gnosticism in, 13; interpretative, 8, 13; Jewish evaluation of, 41f; "keys" to, 13; kinds of in Nietzsche, 93; in Marx, 79–84; methodology in, 5; and methodology in Croce, 128f; as mystery in Maritain, 152; nature of, 1f; objectivity of, 7; and philosophy, 7; philosophy of, 7–16; and positivism, 6; as primarily human, 5; and progress, 66–87; as progress in Teilhard de Chardin, 149; as prophecy, 13; and providence, 12; providential, 143–161; St. Augustine on the progression of, 45; salvation, 43; Schopenhauer on the nonscientific character of, 121; significance of von Ranke in, 124; and subjectivity in Dilthey, 126f; and theology, 12; theory of in Danilevsky, 94–97
Historical methodology, in Croce, 128f
Historicism, 170f
Historiography, nature of Christian, 144
Homology, in Spengler, 101
Horizon analysis, as methodology, 147
Hughes, H. S., 3, 8; on historical objectivity, 6f
Humanitarians, in Marx, 82

Idea, in Hegel, 118
Idealism, 11; Hegelian, 109–119; the nature of, 110; as a thought style, 95; and the thought of Dilthey, 122f
Idiosyncrasy of Spirit, in Hegel, 118
Individual, in Hegel, 116f; in the philosophy of Marx, 80f; in Spengler, 101
Intuition, as methodology in Dilthey, 123
Ionia, and the birth of science, 25
Irenaeus of Lyons, on the nature of history, 38

Janinism, and recurrence, 32
Jaspers, K., on "border situations," 163
Jews, and cyclicism, 41; and history, 39–45
Journet, C., on Maritain, 152

Kant, I., conflict and progress in, 69; and Dilthey, 124; and man's history, 68;

peace and progress in, 69; on the state, 68f; and the theory of progress, 68f
Kluback, W., on Dilthey, 122

Laws of history, in Danilevsky, 96f
Leader, in thought of Hegel, 117
Lewis, C. I., influence of on Danto, 10
Life-philosophy, in Dilthey, 125
Logos, in Heraclitus, 24
Löwith, K., 8f; on the classical conception of time, 21; on cyclicism, 88; on Orosius, 49; on sources of recurrence theory, 11; on Vico, 52
Lubac, H., and the theology of history, 146f

Macquarrie, J., on theology, 147
Man, as historical in Sorokin, 104
Mandala, Buddhist, and recurrence, 32
Mandelbaum, M., on the nature of history, 6
Manuel, F. E., on cyclical and progressive history, 22; on the patristic rejection of cyclicism, 38f; on philosophy of history, 9; on Vico, 51
Maritain, J., on laws in history, 14, 152f; theory of history in, 151ff
Marrou, H., 7; on history as art, 4; on progress, 158f; on secular progress, 158; on Spengler, 98; theory of history in, 158–161
Martyr, J., on the nature of history, 38
Marx, K., on class struggle, 80; criticism of, 84f; and determinism, 81; on the freedom of individuals, 81; and Hegel, 83; on history, 79–84; and humanitarian liberals, 82; influence of Feuerbach on, 80; on laws in nature, 84; on production as an historical determinant, 80; role of the individual in, 80f; and Utopias, 81
Mayo, H. B., on Marx, 84
Meinecke, F., on modes of causality, 170f
Messiah, in Jewish history, 43
Messianism, 44; Davidic, 40f
Metahistory, in Dawson, 157
Metaphysics, bias against in Dilthey, 125f
Methodology, in Dilthey, 123ff; horizon analysis, 147; in Spengler, 101f; of Vico, 55
Mill, J. S., on the influence of Comte, 79
Millenialism, 44
Monism, in Hegel, 115
Morgan, G. A., on Nietzsche's atheism, 91
Murray, J. C., on history, 4
Myth, nature of, 30; and reality, 30

Nationalism, in Spengler, 102
Nations, life of in Hegel, 112

Neo-idealism, as historical methodology, 10

Nietzsche, F., as anti-Christian, 145; atheism in, 91; cyclicism in, 89–94; kinds of history in, 93; on objective truth, 91; opposed to progressivism, 90; the overman in, 92f; on progress, 14; recurrence as fundamental to, 90; revival of recurrence in, 29; theory of history in, 93f; on the ultimacy of change, 92; Will to Power in, 92f

Objective Spirit, in Hegel, 114
Objectivization, in Hegel, 115
Old Testament, and history, 42f
Orosius, P., and the concept of *Romania*, 47; relation of to Augustine, 48f; and salvation history, 49
Otto of Freising, and universal history, 49
Otto, R., on the sense of the holy, 30
Overman, in Nietzsche, 92f

Pantheism, in Dilthey, 125
Past, in Sorokin, 104
Patterns, in history, 14
Perfection, and the circle, 31
Pessimism, in Spengler, 102
Phenomenology, as contemporary mood, 166f
Philo of Alexandria, on the nature of history, 37
Philosophy, role of in Hegel, 119
Philosophy of history, age of, 11; and the analytic tradition, 167; basic categories of, 16; Cohen's definition of, 2; critical and speculative, 10; in Dilthey, 120f; as general orientation, 9; as natural to man, 171f; opposed by Croce, 129f
Plato, on creation, 27; on cyclicism, 25ff; influence of Chaldeans on, 27
Plotinus, and free will, 29
Poetry, nature of Homeric, 31
Polybius, and cyclicism, 37
Popper, K., on Marx, 84; on Plato, 26
Posidonius, and Stoic cosmology, 28
Positivism, as historical methodology, 10
Prefiguration, 38
Production, as an historical determinant in Marx, 80
Progress, and Bacon, 67; in Berdyaev, 85; in Bodin, 70; in Comte, 75–79; in Condorcet, 72ff; a critique of philosophy of, 84f; and the development of philosophy of history, 66; and the Enlightenment, 66; in the French tradition, 67; in Godwin, 73; in Goethe, 69; in Kant, 68f; in Locke, 67; in Marrou, 158f; philosophy of, 14; in Saint-Simon, 74f; and technology, 15; theories of, 15; in Turgot, 70f
Progressivism as nonclassical, 29; opposed by Nietzsche, 90
Pseudohistory, Croce's critique of, 131
Pseudomorphosis, in Spengler, 100
Psychology, and historical knowledge in Dilthey, 121f
Pythagoreans, and cyclicism, 24f

Rahner, K., on eschatology, 147, 160; on theology of history, 143
Ranke, L. von, as historian, 124; influence of on Dilthey, 119; methodology of, 10
Rationalism, opposed in Dilthey, 122f
Recurrence, as fundamental in Nietzsche, 90
Relativism, in Spengler, 99
Religion, as the end of civilization in Toynbee, 139f
Religions, in Toynbee, 138
Renier, G. J., 6
Rite, significance of, 21
Ritschl, F., debt of Nietzsche to, 89
Robinson, J. H., 2; on genetic history, 73
Romanticism, as cultural mood, 169f; and interpretive history, 168f

Sacred, concept of in classical thought, 30
Saint Pierre, on progress, 70
Saint-Simon, H., on the theory of progress, 74f
Samsara, Hindu theory of cycles, 37
Sartre, J. P., on meaning, 164; on Nietzsche, 164f
Saviors, in Toynbee, 137
Schism, of the soul in Toynbee, 137f
Schlesinger, A., Jr., 3
Schopenhauer, A., on Hegel, 111; on the nonscientific character of history, 121
Schroeter, M., on Spengler, 98
Science, birth of, 25
Secularism, as linear, 162
Seneca, modifies Stoic determinism, 29
Shinn, R. L., on Augustine's conception of history, 46
Shotwell, J. T., 3
Simmel, on historical methodology, 121
Sociology, and Comte, 76f
Sorokin, P., 8; change in the thought of, 105; creative altruism in, 107; cultural continuity in, 107; historical character of man in, 104; socio-cultural systems in, 106; theory of history in, 103–107

Spengler, O., 8; critique of, 102f; on cultural decline, 99; on Darwinian progressivism, 101; debt of to Nietzsche and Goethe, 101; destiny in, 100; destiny in history in, 13; Faustian culture in, 102; the individual in, 101; insights of, 13; on linear history, 98; on man, 98; methodology of, 101; and nationalism, 102; pessimism in, 102; prophetism in, 98f; rational analysis in, 100; relativism in, 99; theory of history in, 97–103

State, in Hegel, 111f, 113f; and individual man in Hegel, 113f; in the thought of Dilthey, 127; in Toynbee, 137f

Stern, F., 6

Stoics, and cyclicism, 28; and the theory of periodic conflagration, 24

Subjectivism, in Croce, 128f

Symbol, significance of, 30

Syncretism, in Toynbee, 134, 139f

Talmud, and Jewish history, 44

Taylor, A. E., on the Timaeus, 25

Teilhard de Chardin, P., 8; on civilization, 150; and the end of history, 150f; and the theology of history, 148ff; theory of development in, 150ff

Teleology, in Teilhard de Chardin, 149f

Tertullian, and change, 38

Theology of history, 143–161; ancient character of, 146; basic themes in, 143; Bultmann and, 145; contents of in Rahner, 143; Daniélou on, 160; history of, 144f; Marrou on, 158ff; on Teilhard de Chardin, 148ff; and time, 160

Thompson, J. W., 2

Thucydides, and cyclicism, 37; on recurrence, 88

Timaeus, as furnishing medieval model of nature, 25f

Time, classical conception of, 21, 31; in Vico, 59f

Toynbee, A., 8; against determinism, 136; and analogy, 139; on "challenges," 135f; and Christianity, 141; compared to Spengler, 134; critique of, 141; etherealization in, 136; on Greek historical thought, 30; and Hegel, 139; on the higher religions, 138; idea of the creative minority in, 135f; on the inadequacy of empiricism, 135; and Jung,

140; on nature and growth of civilizations, 135f; on the origin of cyclicism, 11; on religion as the end of civilization, 139f; religious syncretism in, 139f; on schism in body and soul, 137f; the state in, 137f; on theologies, 139; theory of history of, 133–142; and the theory of "saviors," 137

Transcendence, in Hegel, 115f

Turgot, A. R. J., differentiation of nature and history in, 71; and the theory of progress, 70f

Utopias, in Marx, 81

Vico, G., 8; aim of the New Science, 51f; on the barbarism of reflection, 61; and Comte, 60; the corsi and culture in, 62; and cultural continuity, 61f; as cultural historian, 63f; as cultural prophet, 52; on cycle theory, 58–64; dislike of philosophical systems of, 53; and Eastern culture, 63; and empirical science, 56; general critique of, 63f; and historical fallacies, 57; on history, 51–65; last years of, 54; and law, 53; and Leibniz, 64; as litterateur, 54; master plan of the New Science, 55; methodology of the New Science, 55; and mythology, 57; on the nature of ricorso, 62; opposition of to Descartes, 53, 55; and philology, 63; on Plato, 53; on poetry, 53; on political history, 59; and progressivist theory, 62f; publication of the New Science, 54; and Spengler, 59; on temporal periods, 59ff; on time, 59

Vitalism, in Dilthey, 125; in Ortega y Gasset, 164

Voltaire, and contemporary history, 15; as founder of philosophy of history, 67; as interpretative historian, 8

Walsh, W. H., 6, 7, 9; on colligating of events, 13; on impartial history, 7

White, L., 5

White, M., on historical causation, 13

Will to Power, in Nietzsche, 92f

Windelband, on the nature of history, 121

Yantra, Hindu, and recurrence, 32

Zeno, and cyclicism, 28